EVERYMAN, I will go with thee,
and be thy guide,
In thy most need to go by thy side

DYLAN THOMAS

Born at Swansea, 27 October 1914.
Died in New York, 9 November 1953.
Buried at Laugharne, Wales.

DYLAN THOMAS

The Poems

Edited with an introduction and notes by Daniel Jones

Dent: London and Melbourne
EVERYMAN'S LIBRARY

DYLAN THOMAS: THE POEMS

Books by Dylan Thomas

Poems

COLLECTED POEMS, 1934–1952
THE POEMS
SELECTED POEMS

Collections of poems, stories and broadcasts

MISCELLANY ONE
MISCELLANY TWO
MISCELLANY THREE

Prose

COLLECTED STORIES
PORTRAIT OF THE ARTIST AS A YOUNG DOG
ADVENTURES IN THE SKIN TRADE
A PROSPECT OF THE SEA
THE OUTING
HOLIDAY MEMORY
A CHILD'S CHRISTMAS IN WALES
A VISIT TO GRANDPA'S AND OTHER STORIES
COLLECTED LETTERS

———

UNDER MILK WOOD
A Play for Voices

THE COLOUR OF SAYING
An Anthology of Verse Spoken by Dylan Thomas

QUITE EARLY ONE MORNING
A Selection of Radio Scripts by Dylan Thomas

THE DOCTOR AND THE DEVILS
A Film Script

CONTENTS

[**v**]

[vii]

[ix]

APPENDIX I: UNFINISHED POEMS

APPENDIX II: EARLY POEMS

[x]

[xi]

INTRODUCTION

In 1952 Dylan Thomas gathered together eighty-nine of his poems and published them with a specially written Prologue. These were, he said, all he wished to preserve 'up to now'. When Thomas said this, he took for granted that many years of writing lay ahead of him, many new 'Collected Poems' from which even some of the original eighty-nine would perhaps be omitted. But with his death, about a year later, all this changed. For lovers of Thomas's poetry it was no longer a question of 'up to now' with more to follow; it became a question of the significance of everything his short life had allowed him to bequeath to them.

In this book over a hundred poems have been added to the original collection, poems either quite inaccessible or not easily accessible to the reader; as a presentation of Dylan Thomas's contribution to poetry, it is therefore more than twice the size of any previous collection of his work. The order of the poems is the order of composition, as far as I have been able to determine it.

At first sight it might seem that some violence is done here to the 'Collected Poems' by the enlargement of content and the change of order. The *Collected Poems* of 1952 represents Thomas's own choice of content and form under the circumstances and at the time when he made that choice; for this reason, that book will remain significant in its own right. All the 'Collected Poems' are included here, and though they are scattered throughout the book, the original order will be found in the Notes; by consulting them, any reader who feels strongly on the subject can make his own re-arrangement.

This is not, I must emphasize, a collection of the complete poems of Dylan Thomas. In spite of its size, it is still a selection, based upon editorial judgment. I doubt whether any reader could tolerate a lengthy account of my reasons for inclusion or exclusion, but there is one decision I should perhaps explain. I have omitted the poetry of *Under Milk Wood* for two reasons: the play is easily accessible to the public in performance or in print; and the poetry of it, I believe, should be heard or read in the context for which it was intended.

In the preparation of this book I had two principal aims. By including a large amount of additional material I wished to produce a collection of poems more representative of the work of Dylan Thomas as a whole than anything that has yet appeared in one volume; and by arranging the poems in chronological order of composition I hoped to reveal the relationship between poems written at the same time, and the development of the poet in technique and imagery. Here another point can be made, a point to which the reader can assign a small or a great degree of importance, according to his taste. A poet does not live in a vacuum; he is influenced by what happens to him and to others, by contemporary thought, contemporary art, the changing of the seasons, and the environment in which he lives. These influences emerge clearly from a chronological presentation of his work. To give one example only, the later poems of Dylan Thomas are full of reference to, or imagery derived from, the water-birds and the birds of prey he saw in such numbers from the window of the hut where he worked, overlooking the Laugharne estuary.

Many of the additional poems appeared during Thomas's lifetime in periodicals and anthologies, but many, including the two unfinished poems in Appendix I, were still in manuscript at the time of his death.

The first of the unfinished poems, 'In Country Heaven', I have reconstructed from manuscripts supplied to me by the University of Texas; other reconstructions could, I know, be made from the same or from other material, and I make no claim that my version is necessarily the best.

The second unfinished poem, 'Elegy', skilfully reconstructed by Vernon Watkins, was published three years after the death of Dylan Thomas in *Encounter* (XXIX, pp. 30–1).

A rich source of material unpublished in the poet's lifetime is the mixed collection presented to the British Museum in 1954 by Mr Trevor Hughes (Add. MSS. 48217). I call the collection 'mixed' because, while some poems are wholly in Thomas's handwriting, in some he has written only the title, the rest of the text being in typescript; about four different typewriters were used, presumably including Mr Hughes's, Pamela Hansford Johnson's, and my own. The eight completely typewritten poems on folios 54, 55, and 58 to 63 in the Hughes Collection are collaborations; in them, Thomas composed only the even-numbered lines. A note about this has now been inserted in the manuscript by Mr T. C. Skeat, Keeper of Manuscripts, the British Museum.

Dylan Thomas's fondness for collaboration, especially in the early years, has created a trap into which many students of his work, including commentators and bibliographers, have fallen; such poems have sometimes been printed as if they were his alone, and academic structures have been built upon the error. Prose collaboration between us was comparatively rare, but between 1930 and 1934 about two hundred poems were written in collaboration, with Thomas supplying the even-numbered lines only; I wrote the odd ones. Most of these survive in manuscripts that clearly show the alternation of our handwriting; but, because Thomas was at the time ashamed of his print-like lettering, some are wholly copied out by me, and a few are typewritten. This collaboration extends even to three or four poems that appeared in the *Swansea Grammar School Magazine* above the initials 'D.M.T.' Conversely, many poems in the same magazine which have never been ascribed to Thomas, are in fact by him. Poems written in collaboration are excluded from this book.

The task of establishing the date of composition varied in difficulty. Sometimes the date was supplied by Thomas himself; sometimes a date, or at least an approximate date, could be deduced from letters or other sources. When all else has failed, I have allowed myself to be guided by the date of first publication. This method is not as fallacious as it may seem. When Thomas was satisfied that a poem had reached its final form, he was always anxious—for several reasons—to see it in print as soon as possible.

Recognition came easily and early to him, and, with recognition, the rejection of a poem by a periodical seldom occurred, if ever. In any case, it is surely more important to estimate the order in which the poems were written than to establish precise dates of composition. These two things are not by any means inseparable. It is often possible, for example, to make a reasonable conjecture about the time of composition of an undated poem, if it can be shown that it was preceded and followed by other poems the dates of which are known.

Chronological arrangement of the poems brings out many interesting aspects of the poet's work: for example, the relation of poems written in groups within short periods, and the fluctuation in quantity of output from year to year.

On the eve of a one-man exhibition an artist often will paint hurriedly, but with great intensity, a few more canvases to cover empty spaces on the gallery walls, perhaps to link together or to contrast with work already done; in the same way, imminent publication of a new volume of poetry would stimulate Thomas, or would force him, to produce more—and more of a certain kind, within a short space of time. Just before *Eighteen Poems* (1934), *Twenty-five Poems* (1936), *The Map of Love* (1939), *New Poems* (1943) and *Deaths and Entrances* (1946), Thomas wrote groups of new poems, or exerted himself to revise old ones.

Extensive revision of earlier verse was always a regular feature of the poet's working method. In the four years between 1930 and 1934 he wrote at least four times more poetry than in the remaining nineteen years of his life. This huge body of poems became a store from which he drew constantly almost to the very end. Sometimes a poem was taken whole from the store and produced almost without alteration years later, but more often it underwent significant revision at one stage or at several stages. In cases of this kind, it has been by no means easy to decide upon a date of composition.

There is a time when a poem emerges in its essence; this may be at, or near, the beginning of composition, or at one of many stages of revision. As a generalization, or as an abstraction, a poem 'in its 'essence' cannot be defined; it can only be recognized as an experience limited to each poem. The experience is positive, but recognition of it can be supported only by negative proofs, for example, by the way in which the poem survives, or does not survive, alterations of words or word-order, changes of syntax or punctuation, deletions or additions. Where a choice has been forced upon me, I have had to use my own judgment in recognizing the moment when the essential poem has come into being, the moment when, in spite of its complex evolution, a virtually new poem has been composed, more closely related to the final text than to its origins; this I have taken to be the time of composition of the poem as it appears in this book.

Textual decisions, apart from the texts of the unfinished poems, have presented less difficulty, but it would be misleading to pretend that there is no difficulty at all. At first sight, it would seem to be merely a question of finding out which text Dylan Thomas himself had last seen, and therefore presumably had approved, and of using that. But there are many fallacies involved here. In the first place, this assumes that Thomas was infallible in proof-reading and in the detection of errors. He was good, but not infallible. Publishers, printers, friends and unknown readers sometimes drew his attention to errors in work already published, and after his death still others were noted. In the course of time, it is true, this tended to have a 'sieving' effect, the errors becoming more and more insignificant. On the other hand, it must be remembered that many of the poems in this collection remained unpublished during the poet's lifetime; these, therefore, were never finally revised, prepared for publication or proof-read. To add to these difficulties, the style of Thomas's writing sometimes presents problems of interpretation, for example in syntax and punctuation, and even in grammar and spelling. I have dealt with these difficulties as well as I can, and that is all I can say.

The poem 'Prologue', written in August 1952, stands outside the chronological form of the book. Written specially for the *Collected Poems*, it rightly takes first place here, even though it was the last poem, apart from poems in *Under Milk Wood*, that Dylan

Thomas completed. In Appendix II, *Early Poems*, the composition of the poems extends from 1926 to 1930; the earliest poem was written by Thomas when he was eleven years of age. Between the last poem of Appendix II and the first poem of the main body of poems ('I know this vicious minute's hour'), Thomas had just passed his sixteenth birthday. The one hundred and sixty-three poems in the main body of the book extend from November 1930 to October 1951. The reader who prefers to take all the poems in strictly chronological order, from the poet's eleventh birthday to his death, should therefore read them in this order: Appendix II, Poems 1 to 163, Prologue, Appendix I.

In the Notes I have tried to restrict myself to dates, sources and publications, adding a commentary only when I thought it indispensable. This is as Thomas himself would have wished. On the other hand, I believe he would have forgiven me for my long Note on Verse-Patterns (page 245), and I flatter myself he might even have applauded my Note on 'Altarwise by owl-light' (page 262), which amounts to a rebuttal of the charge of 'obscurity', or—to be precise—the expression of a personal view that, as far as this particular poet is concerned—not by any means as far as many other poets are concerned—the whole question is irrelevant.

I am indebted to the University of Texas and Mrs Mary M. Hirth, Librarian at the Academic Center there, for supplying me with photographic copies of Dylan Thomas manuscripts, and to Mr T. C. Skeat, Keeper of Manuscripts at the British Museum, and the officials of the British Museum Department of Periodicals at Colindale, for their help. I am grateful to Mrs Gwendoline Watkins for permission to print the reconstruction of 'Elegy', and to my son, the poet's godson, Dylan Jones, for his secretarial work.

All students of Dylan Thomas owe much, of course, to the work of Professor Ralph Maud. His *Poet in the Making* proved most useful to me in establishing the date of composition of poems written between April 1930 and August 1933 from notebooks to which he had access in the Lockwood Memorial Library, Buffalo, N.Y. I wish to pay special tribute here to the Professor for his meticulous editing of the notebook texts and for his thoughtful and scholarly introduction to them.

Dylan Thomas: A Bibliography, by J. Alexander Rolph, helped to guide me through the maze of periodicals in which some of the poems were first published. Finally I found valuable information about the dates and the circumstances of composition of several poems in Constantine FitzGibbon's *The Life of Dylan Thomas* and *Selected Letters of Dylan Thomas*, and in Vernon Watkins's *Dylan Thomas: Letters to Vernon Watkins*.

DANIEL JONES

June 1970

NOTE ON THE 1978 PRINTING

The new printing includes a poem recently discovered, and never before published in any anthology. Accidentally found by Wynford Vaughan Thomas, in whose presence most of the lines were written, the poem is an amusing specimen of the sort of 'pub verse' in which Thomas indulged.

January 1978

PROLOGUE

PROLOGUE

This day winding down now
At God speeded summer's end
In the torrent salmon sun,
In my seashaken house
On a breakneck of rocks
Tangled with chirrup and fruit,
Froth, flute, fin and quill
At a wood's dancing hoof,
By scummed, starfish sands
With their fishwife cross
Gulls, pipers, cockles, and sails,
Out there, crow black, men
Tackled with clouds, who kneel
To the sunset nets,
Geese nearly in heaven, boys
Stabbing, and herons, and shells
That speak seven seas,
Eternal waters away
From the cities of nine
Days' night whose towers will catch
In the religious wind
Like stalks of tall, dry straw,
At poor peace I sing
To you strangers (though song
Is a burning and crested act,
The fire of birds in
The world's turning wood,
For my sawn, splay sounds),
Out of these seathumbed leaves
That will fly and fall
Like leaves of trees and as soon
Crumble and undie
Into the dogdayed night.
Seaward the salmon, sucked sun slips,

And the dumb swans drub blue
My dabbed bay's dusk, as I hack
This rumpus of shapes
For you to know
How I, a spinning man,
Glory also this star, bird
Roared, sea born, man torn, blood blest.
Hark: I trumpet the place,
From fish to jumping hill! Look:
I build my bellowing ark
To the best of my love
As the flood begins,
Out of the fountainhead
Of fear, rage red, manalive,
Molten and mountainous to stream
Over the wound asleep
Sheep white hollow farms

To Wales in my arms.
Hoo, there, in castle keep,
You king singsong owls, who moonbeam
The flickering runs and dive
The dingle furred deer dead!
Huloo, on plumbed bryns,
O my ruffled ring dove
In the hooting, nearly dark
With Welsh and reverent rook,
Coo rooing the woods' praise,
Who moons her blue notes from her nest
Down to the curlew herd!
Ho, hullaballoing clan
Agape, with woe
In your beaks, on the gabbing capes!
Heigh, on horseback hill, jack
Whisking hare! who
Hears, there, this fox light, my flood ship's

Clangour as I hew and smite
(A clash of anvils for my
Hubbub and fiddle, this tune
On a tongued puffball)
But animals thick as thieves
On God's rough tumbling grounds
(Hail to His beasthood).
Beasts who sleep good and thin,
Hist, in hogsback woods! The haystacked
Hollow farms in a throng
Of waters cluck and cling,
And barnroofs cockcrow war!
O kingdom of neighbours, finned
Felled and quilled, flash to my patch
Work ark and the moonshine
Drinking Noah of the bay,
With pelt, and scale, and fleece:
Only the drowned deep bells
Of sheep and churches noise
Poor peace as the sun sets
And dark shoals every holy field.
We will ride out alone, and then,
Under the stars of Wales,
Cry, Multitudes of arks! Across
The water lidded lands,
Manned with their loves they'll move,
Like wooden islands, hill to hill.
Huloo, my prowed dove with a flute!
Ahoy, old, sea-legged fox,
Tom tit and Dai mouse!
My ark sings in the sun
At God speeded summer's end
And the flood flowers now.

THE POEMS

I KNOW THIS VICIOUS MINUTE'S HOUR

I know this vicious minute's hour;
It is a sour motion in the blood,
That, like a tree, has roots in you,
And buds in you.
Each silver moment chimes
    in steps of sound,
And I, caught in mid-air perhaps,
Hear and am still the little bird.
You have offended, periodic heart;
You I shall drown unreasonably,
Leave you in me to be found
Darker than ever,
Too full with blood to let my love flow in.
Stop is unreal;
I want reality to hold
    within my palm,
Not, as a symbol, stone
    speaking or no,
But it, reality, whose voice I know
To be the circle not the stair of sound.
Go is my wish;
Then shall I go,
But in the light of going
Minutes are mine
I could devote to other things.
Stop has no minutes,
    but I go or die.

COOL, OH NO COOL

Cool, oh no cool,
Sharp, oh no sharp,
The hillock of the thoughts you think
With that half-moulded mind I said was yours,
But cooler when I take it back,
And sharper if I break asunder
The icicle of each deliberate fancy.
For when I bought you for a thought, (you cost no more)
How could I smooth that skin
Knowing a dream could darken it,
And, the string pulled, some mental doll
Ravage and break,
How kiss, when doll could say
Master, her mouth is sawdust
And her tongue, look, ash,
   Part from her,
   Part from her,
Sweet, automatic me knows best.
But you shall not go from me, creation;
Oh no, my mind is your panopticon;
You shall not go unless I will it
And my thoughts flow so uneasily
There is no measured sea for them,
No place in which, wave perched on wave,
Such energy may gain
The sense it is to have.
You wish to stay my prisoner
Closed in your cell of secret thoughts,
And I, your captor, have my love to keep
From which you may not fly.

THE AIR YOU BREATHE

The air you breathe encroaches
The throat is mine I know the neck
Wind is my enemy your hair shant stir
Under his strong impulsive kiss
The rainbow's foot is not more apt
To have the centaur lover
So steal her not O goat-legged wind
But leave but still adore
For if the gods would love
Theyd see with eyes like mine
But should not touch like I
Your sweet inducive thighs
And raven hair.

4

CABARET

I, poor romantic, held her heel
Upon the island of my palm,
And saw towards her tiny face
Going her glistening calves that minute.
There was a purpose in her pointed foot;
Her thighs and underclothes were sweet,
And drew my spiral breath
To circumambulate for decency
Their golden and their other colour.
The band was playing on the balcony.
One lady's hand was lifted,
But she did not cry, 'I see;
I see the man is mad with love.'
Her fan burst in a million lights

As that her heel was lifted,
Gone from my palm to leave it marked
With quite a kind of heart.
She is on dancing toes again,
Sparkling a twelve-legged body
And many arms to raise
Over her heel and me.
I, poor romantic, contemplate
The insect on this painted tree.
Which is the metal wing
And which the real?

5

SOMETIMES THE SKY'S TOO BRIGHT

Sometimes the sky's too bright,
Or has too many clouds or birds,
And far away's too sharp a sun
To nourish thinking of him.
Why is my hand too blunt
To cut in front of me
My horrid images for me,
Of over-fruitful smiles,
The weightless touching of the lip
I wish to know
I cannot lift, but can,
The creature with the angel's face
Who tells me hurt,
And sees my body go
Down into misery?
No stopping. Put the smile
Where tears have come to dry.
The angel's hurt is left;
His telling burns.

Sometimes a woman's heart has salt,
Or too much blood;
I tear her breast,
And see the blood is mine,
Flowing from her but mine,
And then I think
Perhaps the sky's too bright;
And watch my hand,
But do not follow it,
And feel the pain it gives,
But do not ache.

6

RAIN CUTS THE PLACE WE TREAD

Rain cuts the place we tread,
A sparkling fountain for us
With no fountain boy but me
To balance on my palms
The water from a street of clouds.
We sail a boat upon the path,
Paddle with leaves
Down an ecstatic line of light,
Watching, not too aware
To make our senses take too much,
The unrolled waves
So starred with gravel,
The living vessels of the garden
Drifting in easy time;
And, as we watch, the rainbow's foot
Stamps on the ground,
A legendary horse with hoof and feather,
Impatient to be off.
He goes across the sky,

But, when he's out of sight,
The mark his flying tail has left
Branches a million shades,
A gay parabola
Above a boat of leaves and weeds.
We try to steer;
The stream's fantastically hard,
Too stiff to churn with leaves,
A sedge of broken stalks and shells.
This is a drain of iron plants,
For when we touch a flower with our oar
We strike but do not stir it.
Our boat is made to rise
By waves which grow again
Their own melodious height,
Into the rainbow's shy embrace.
We shiver uncomplainingly,
And taste upon our lips, this minute,
The emerald kiss,
And breath on breath of indigo.

7

THE MORNING, SPACE FOR LEDA

The morning, space for Leda
To stir the water with a buoyant foot,
And interlude for violins
To catch her sailing down the stream—
The phrases on the wood aren't hers;
A fishing bird has notes of ivory
Alive within his craning throat—
Sees the moon still up,
Bright, well-held head,
And, for a pivot,

The shadows from the glassy sea
To wet the sky with tears,
And daub the unrisen sun with longing.
The swan makes strings of water in her wake;
Between the moon and sun
There's time to pluck a tune upon the harp,
Moisten the mouth of sleep
To kiss awake
My hand with honey that had closed upon a flower.
Between the rising and the falling
Spring may be green—
Under her cloth of trees no sorrow,
Under her grassy dress no limbs—
And winter follow like an echo
The summer voice so warm from fruit
That clustered round her shoulders,
And hid her uncovered breast.
The morning, too, is time for love,
When Leda, on a toe of down,
Dances a measure with the swan
Who holds her clasped inside his strong, white wings;
And darkness, hand in hand with light,
Is blind with tears too frail to taste.

8

THE SPIRE CRANES

The spire cranes. Its statue is an aviary.
From the stone nest it does not let the feathery
Carved birds blunt their striking throats on the salt gravel,
Pierce the spilt sky with diving wing in weed and heel
An inch in froth. Chimes cheat the prison spire, pelter
In time like outlaw rains on that priest, water,
Time for the swimmers' hands, music for silver lock

And mouth. Both note and plume plunge from the spire's hook.
Those craning birds are choice for you, songs that jump back
To the built voice, or fly with winter to the bells,
But do not travel down dumb wind like prodigals.

9

TIME ENOUGH TO ROT

Time enough to rot;
Toss overhead
Your golden ball of blood;
Breathe against air,
Puffing the light's flame to and fro,
Not drawing in your suction's kiss.
Your mouth's fine dust
Will find such love against the grain,
And break through dark;
It's acrid in the streets;
A paper witch upon her sulphured broom
Flies from the gutter.
The still go hard,
The moving fructify;
The walker's apple's black as sin;
The waters of his mind draw in.
    Then swim your head,
    For you've a sea to lie.

10

IT'S NOT IN MISERY BUT IN OBLIVION

It's not in misery but in oblivion,
Not vertically in a mood of joy
Screaming the spring

Over the ancient winter,
He'll lie down, and our breath
Will chill the roundness of his cheeks,
And make his wide mouth home.
For we must whisper down the funnel
The love we had and glory in his blood
Coursing along the channels
Until the spout dried up
That flowed out of the soil
All seasons with the same meticulous power,
But the veins must fail.
He's not awake to the grave
Though we cry down the funnel,
Splitting a thought into such hideous moments
As drown, over and over, this fever.
He's dead, home, has no lover,
But our speaking does not thrive
In the bosom, or the empty channels.
Our evil, when we breathe it,
Of dissolution and the empty fall,
Won't harm the tent around him,
Uneaten and not to be pierced
By us in sin or us in gaiety.
And who shall tell the amorist
Oblivion is so loverless.

II

THE NATURAL DAY AND NIGHT

The natural day and night
Are full enough to drown my melancholy
Of sound and sight,
Vigour and harmony in light to none,

One hour spend my time for me
In tuning impulses to calls;
Kinder;
So phrase;
Don't hurt the chic anatomy
Of ladies' needles worn to breaking point
Sewing a lie to a credulity,
With zest culled from their ladylike heat,
Hedgerow, laboratory, and even glasshouse,
But the sun cracks it
But the stones crack it
Out of my hand in stopping up my mouth,
My ears, my nose, my eyes,
And all my thin prerogative of taste.
But while day is there's night to it,
And night to it.
The black shadow comes down,
And the beautiful noise is quelled,
For my merry words,
So rare—
Who taught me trouble?
I, said the beetle, out of my thin black womb,
Out of my thin black lips,
Trouble enough for the world
Out of my filthy eyes
And my corrupting knowledge—
They are words for weeping.
Crying aloud in pain,
Thick to the skull,
Oh gaiety!
Oh gaiety!
Penumbra derry,
Do the right thing to do the right;
Do, down a derry.

CONCEIVE THESE IMAGES IN AIR

Conceive these images in air,
Wrap them in flame, they're mine;
Set against granite,
Let the two dull stones be grey,
Or, formed of sand,
Trickle away through thought,
In water or in metal,
Flowing and melting under lime.
Cut them in rock,
So, not to be defaced,
They harden and take shape again
As signs I've not brought down
To any lighter state
By love-tip or my hand's red heat.

THE NEOPHYTE, BAPTIZED IN SMILES

The neophyte, baptized in smiles,
Is laughing boy beneath his oath,
Breathing no poison from the oval mouth,
Or evil from the cankered heart.
Where love is there's a crust of joy
To hide what drags its belly from the egg,
And, on the ground, gyrates as easily
As though the sun were spinning up through it.
Boy sucks no sweetness from the willing mouth,
Nothing but poison from the breath,
And, in the grief of certainty,

Knows his love rots.
Outdo your prude's genetic faculty
That grew for good
Out of the bitter conscience and the nerves,
Not from the senses' dualizing tip
Of water, flame, or air.
Wetten your tongue and lip,
Moisten your care to carelessness,
For she who sprinkled on your brow
Soft shining symbols of her peace with you,
Was old when you were young,
Old in illusions turned to acritudes,
And thoughts, be they so kind,
Touched, by a finger's nail, to dust.

14

TO BE ENCOMPASSED BY THE BRILLIANT EARTH

To be encompassed by the brilliant earth
Breathing on all sides pungently
Into her vegetation's lapping mouths
Must feel like such encroachment
As edges off your nerves to mine,
The hemming contact that's so trammelled
By love or look,
In death or out of death,
Glancing from the yellow nut,
Eyeing from the wax's tower,
Or, white as milk, out of the seeping dark,
The drooping as you close me in
A world of webs
I touch and break,
I touch and break.

[20]

ALTHOUGH THROUGH MY BEWILDERED WAY

Although through my bewildered way
Of crying off this unshaped evil,
Death to the magical when all is done,
Age come to you—you're bright and useless,
Soon to my care, my love,
But soon to die
In time, like all, through my unreason
In a gay moment's falsity—
There is no need of hope for hope,
You'll bring the place to me
Where all is well,
Noble among a crowd of lights.
Then shall your senses, out of joy,
Tingle on mine;
You're the perverse to lie across,
Out of the heart for me,
Sick, pale, and plain,
So that the process calls for laughs,
The silly binding
Snapped in a rain of pieces falling
On head and running foot,
For, if I could, I'd fly away,
For, if I could, I'd fly away
Before the last light is blown
Into the void again of this bewilderment and that insanity

16

HIGH ON A HILL

High on a hill,
Straddle and soak,
Out of the way of the eyes of men,

Out of the way,
Straddle her wrinkled knees
Until the day's broken—
Christ, let me write from the heart,
War on the heart—
Puff till the adder is,
Breathe till the snake is home,
Inch on the old thigh
Till the bird has burst his shell,
And the carnal stem that stood
Blowing with the blood's ebb,
Is fallen down
To the ground.

17

SINCE, ON A QUIET NIGHT

Since, on a quiet night, I heard them talk
Who have no voices but the winds'
Of all the mystery there is in life
And all the mastery there is in death,
I have not lain an hour asleep
But troubled by their curious speech
Stealing so softly into the ears.
One says: There was a woman with no friend,
And, standing over the sea, she'd cry
Her loneliness across the empty waves
Time after time.
And every voice:
Oblivion is as loverless;
Oblivion is as loverless.
And then again: There was a child
Upon the earth who knew no joy,
For there was no light in his eyes,
And there was no light in his soul.

Oblivion is as blind,
Oblivion is as blind,
I hear them say out of the darkness
Who have no talk but that of death.

THEY ARE THE ONLY DEAD WHO DID NOT LOVE

They are the only dead who did not love,
Lipless and tongueless in the sour earth
Staring at others, poor unlovers.
They are the only living thing who did love,
So are we full with strength,
Ready to rise, easy to sleep.
Who has completeness that can cut
A comic hour to an end through want of woman
And the warmth she gives,
And yet be human,
Feel the same soft blood flow thoroughly,
Have food and drink, unloving?
None, and his deadly welcome
At the hour's end
Shall prove unworthy for his doing,
Which was good at word,
But came from out the mouth unknowing
Of such great goodness as is ours.
There is no dead but is not loved
Awhile, a little,
Out of the fullness of another's heart
Having so much to spare.
That, then, is fortunate,
But, by your habit unreturned,
And by your habit unreturnable.
So is there missed a certain godliness
That's not without its woe,

And not without divinity,
For it can quicken or it can kill.
Look, there's the dead who did not love,
And there's the living who did love,
Around our little selves
Touching our separate love with badinage

19

LITTLE PROBLEM

Foot, head, or traces
Are on sandy soil their spirit level;
Their level is the length
Of foot on head we'll be the time
In tracing
For a purpose (head to foot is head and foot,
    No wit, is one),
That'll make, it's brittle, diaphragm
For use of sense, (no hurt no sense).
Foot head compressed,
It's easy tracing what each gives the other
By toe or hair to common good,
    (Good for can run
    And know why run),
Though, after's done, I
See the reason for undoubling doubling not,
Unless for poetry, which, if it asks me
For a spirit, can
Run and know why
And know why know, no wit,
Can ever further,
Though no ask brings it
For a lazy sake that won't create
But only plumb such depths
As you, Original, derive.

WHEN YOU HAVE GROUND SUCH BEAUTY DOWN TO DUST

When you have ground such beauty down to dust
As flies before the breath
And, at the touch, trembles with lover's fever,
Or sundered it to look the closer,
Magnified and made immense
At one side's loss,
Turn inside out, and see at glance
Wisdom is folly, love is not,
Sense can but maim it, wisdom mar it,
Folly purify and make it true.
For folly was
When wisdom lay not in the soul
But in the body of the trees and stones,
Was when sense found a way to them
Growing on hills or shining under water.
Come wise in foolishness,
Go silly and be Christ's good brother,
He whose lovers were both wise and sensible
When folly stirred, warm in the foolish heart.

THERE'S PLENTY IN THE WORLD

There's plenty in the world that doth not die,
And much that lives to perish,
That rises and then falls, buds but to wither;
The season's sun, though he should know his setting
Up to the second of the dark coming,
Death sights and sees with great misgiving
A rib of cancer on the fluid sky.

But we, shut in the houses of the brain,
Brood on each hothouse plant
Spewing its sapless leaves around,
And watch the hand of time unceasingly
Ticking the world away,
Shut in the madhouse call for cool air to breathe.
There's plenty that doth die;
Time cannot heal nor resurrect;
And yet, mad with young blood or stained with age,
We still are loth to part with what remains,
Feeling the wind about our heads that does not cool,
And on our lips the dry mouth of the rain.

22

WRITTEN FOR A PERSONAL EPITAPH

Feeding the worm
Who do I blame
Because laid down
At last by time,
Here under the earth with girl and thief,
Who do I blame?
Mother I blame
Whose loving crime
Moulded my form
Within her womb,
Who gave me life and then the grave,
Mother I blame.
Here is her labour's end,
Dead limb and mind,
All love and sweat
Gone now to rot.
I am man's reply to every question,
His aim and destination.

NEVER TO REACH THE OBLIVIOUS DARK

Never to reach the oblivious dark
And not to know
Any man's troubles nor your own—
Negatives impress negation,
Empty of light and find the darkness lit—
Never is nightmare,
Never flows out from the wound of sleep
Staining the broken brain
With knowledge that no use and nothing worth
Still's vain to argue after death;
No use to run your head against the wall
To find a sweet blankness in the blood and shell,
This pus runs deep.
There's poison in your red wine, drinker,
Which spreads down to the dregs
Leaving a corrupted vein of colour,
Sawdust beneath the skirts;
On every hand the evil's positive
For dead or live,
Froth or a moment's movement
All hold the sum, nothing to nothing,
Even the words are nothing
While the sun's turned to salt,
Can be but vanity, such an old cry,
Nothing never, nothing older
Though we're consumed by loves and doubts.
I love and doubt, it's vain, it's vain,
Loving and doubting like one who is to die
Planning what's good, though it's but winter,
When spring is come,
The jonquil and the trumpet.

CHILDREN OF DARKNESS GOT NO WINGS

Children of darkness got no wings,
This we know we got no wings,
Stay, dramatic figures, tethered down
By weight of cloth and fact,
Crystal or funeral, got no hope
For us that knows misventure
Only as wrong; but shan't the genius fail,
Gliding, rope-dancing, is his fancy,
Better nor us can't gainsay walking,
Who'll break our necks upon the pavement
Easier than he upon the ice.
For we are ordinary men,
Sleep, wake, and sleep, eat, love, and laugh,
With wide, dry mouths and eyes,
Poor, petty vermin,
Stink of cigarettes and armpits,
Cut our figures, and retreat at night
Into a double or a single bed,
The same thoughts in our head.
We are ordinary men,
Bred in the dark behind the skirting-board,
Crying with hungry voices in our nest.

Children of darkness got no wings,
This we know, we got no wings,
Stay, in a circle chalked upon the floor,
Waiting all vainly this we know.

TOO LONG, SKELETON

Too long, skeleton, death's risen
Out of the soil and seed into the drive,
Chalk cooled by leaves in the hot season,
Too long, skeleton, death's all alive
From nape to toe, a sanatorium piece
Sly as an adder, rid of fleas.
Take now content, no longer posturing
As raped and reaped, the final emblem.
Thy place is filled, bones bid for auction,
The prism of the eye now void by suction,
New man best whose blood runs thick,
Rather than charnel-house as symbol
Of the moment and the dead hour.

NEARLY SUMMER

Nearly summer, and the devil
Still comes visiting his poor relations,
If not in person sends his unending evil
By messengers, the flight of birds
Spelling across the sky his devil's news,
The seasons' cries, full of his intimations.
He has the whole field now, the gods departed
Who cannot count the seeds he sows,
The law allows
His wild carouses, and his lips
Poised at the ready ear
To whisper, when he wants, the senses' war

Or lay the senses' rumour.
The welcome devil comes as guest,
Steals what is best—the body's splendour—
Rapes, leaves for lost (the amorist!),
Counts on his fist
All he has reaped in wonder.

The welcome devil comes invited,
Suspicious but that soon passes.
They cry to be taken, and the devil breaks
All that is not already broken,
Leaves it among the cigarette ends and the glasses.

27

YOUTH CALLS TO AGE

You too have seen the sun a bird of fire
Stepping on clouds across the golden sky,
Have known man's envy and his weak desire,
Have loved and lost.
You, who are old, have loved and lost as I
All that is beautiful but born to die,
Have traced your patterns in the hastening frost.
And you have walked upon the hills at night,
And bared your head beneath the living sky,
When it was noon have walked into the light,
Knowing such joy as I.
Though there are years between us, they are naught;
Youth calls to age across the tired years:
'What have you found,' he cries, 'what have you sought?'
'What you have found,' age answers through his tears,
'What you have sought.'

BEING BUT MEN

Being but men, we walked into the trees
Afraid, letting our syllables be soft
For fear of waking the rooks,
For fear of coming
Noiselessly into a world of wings and cries.

If we were children we might climb,
Catch the rooks sleeping, and break no twig,
And, after the soft ascent,
Thrust out our heads above the branches
To wonder at the unfailing stars.

Out of confusion, as the way is,
And the wonder that man knows,
Out of the chaos would come bliss.

That, then, is loveliness, we said,
Children in wonder watching the stars,
Is the aim and the end.

Being but men, we walked into the trees.

OUT OF THE SIGHS

Out of the sighs a little comes,
But not of grief, for I have knocked down that
Before the agony; the spirit grows,
Forgets, and cries;
A little comes, is tasted and found good;

All could not disappoint;
There must, be praised, some certainty,
If not of loving well, then not,
And that is true after perpetual defeat.

After such fighting as the weakest know,
There's more than dying;
Lose the great pains or stuff the wound,
He'll ache too long
Through no regret of leaving woman waiting
For her soldier stained with spilt words
That spill such acrid blood.

Were that enough, enough to ease the pain,
Feeling regret when this is wasted
That made me happy in the sun,
How much was happy while it lasted,
Were vaguenesses enough and the sweet lies plenty,
The hollow words could bear all suffering
And cure me of ills.

Were that enough, bone, blood, and sinew,
The twisted brain, the fair-formed loin,
Groping for matter under the dog's plate,
Man should be cured of distemper.
For all there is to give I offer:
Crumbs, barn, and halter.

30

UPON YOUR HELD-OUT HAND

Upon your held-out hand
Count the endless days until they end,
Feel, as the pulse grows tired,

The angels' wings beating about your head
Unsounding, they beat so soft.
Why count so sadly?
Learn to be merry with the merriest,
Or (change the key!) give vent to utterances
As meaningless as the bells (oh change the life!),
The sideboard fruit, the ferns, the picture houses
And the pack of cards.

When I was seven I counted four and forty trees
That stood before my window,
Which may or may not be relevant
And symbolise the maddening factors
That madden both watchers and actors.
I've said my piece: count or go mad.
The new asylum on the hill
Leers down the valley like a fool
Waiting and watching for your fingers to fail
To keep count of the stiles
The thousand sheep
Leap over to my criss-cross rhythms.
I've said my piece.

31

WALKING IN GARDENS

Walking in gardens by the sides
Of marble bathers toeing the garden ponds,
Skirting the ordered beds of paint-box flowers,
We spoke of drink and girls, for hours
Touched on the outskirts of the mind,
Then stirred a little chaos in the sun.
A new divinity, a god of wheels
Destroying souls and laying waste,

Trampling to dust the bits and pieces
Of faulty men and their diseases,
Rose in our outworn brains. We spoke our lines,
Made, for the bathers to admire,
Dramatic gestures in the air.
Ruin and revolution
Whirled in our words, then faded.
We might have tried light matches in the wind.
Over and round the ordered garden hummed,
There was no need of a new divinity,
No tidy flower moved, no bather gracefully
Lifted her marble foot, or lowered her hand
To brush upon the waters of the pond.

32

NOW THE THIRST PARCHES LIP AND TONGUE

Now the thirst parches lip and tongue,
The dry fever burns until no heart is left,
Now is decay in bone and sinew,
When heaven—open wide the gates—has taken flight,
Searing the sky for thunderbolts to fall
On man and mountain,
Is treason's time and the time of envy.

The acid pours away, the acid drips
Into the places and the crevices
Most fit for lovers to make harmony,
To catch the lovers' palsy,
And on the sweethearts' bed to lie and grin,
To smirk at love's undress,
Make mock of woman's meat,
And drown all sorrows in the gross catastrophe.

[34]

LIFT UP YOUR FACE

Lift up your face, light
Breaking, stare at the sky
Consoling for night by day
That chases the ghosts of the trees
And the ghosts of the brain,
Making fresh what was stale
In the unsleeping mummery
Of men and creatures horribly
Staring at stone walls.
Lift up your head, let
Comfort come through the devil's clouds,
The nightmare's mist
Suspended from the devil's precipice,
Let comfort come slowly, lift
Up your hand to stroke the light,
Its honeyed cheek, soft-talking mouth,
Lift up the blinds over the blind eyes.

Out of unsleeping cogitations,
When the skeleton of war
Is with the corpse of peace,
(Notes not in sympathy, discord, unease),
The only visitor,
Must come content.
Therefore lift up, see, stroke the light.
Content shall come after a twisted night
If only with sunlight.

LET IT BE KNOWN

Let it be known that little live but lies,
Love-lies, and god-lies, and lies-to-please,
Let children know, and old men at their gates,
That this is lies that moans departure,
And that is lies that, after the old men die,
Declare their souls, let children know, live after.

THE MIDNIGHT ROAD

The midnight road, though young men tread unknowing,
Harbouring some thought of heaven, or haven hoping,
Yields peace and plenty at the end. Or is it peace,
This busy jarring on the nerves yet no outbreak?
And this is plenty, then, cloves and sweet oils, the bees' honey,
Enough kind food, enough kind speaking,
A film of people moving,
Their hands outstretched, to give and give?
And now behind the screen are vixen voices,
The midnight figures of a sulphurous brood
Stepping in nightmare on a nightmare's edges.
Above them poise the swollen clouds
That wait for breaking and that never break,
The living sky, the faces of the stars.

WITH WINDMILLS TURNING WRONG DIRECTIONS

With windmills turning wrong directions,
And signposts pointing up and down

Towards destruction and redemption,
No doubt the wind on which the rooks
Tumble, not flying, is false,
Plays scurvy tricks with values and intentions,
Guides and blows wickedly, for larks
Find hard to dart against a cloud,
To London's turned, and thirsty loads
Of men with flannel shirts
And girls with flowered hats
Intent on visiting the famous spots,
Ride in their charabancs on roads
That lead away to dirty towns
Dirtier with garages and cheap tea signs.

Faith in divinity would solve most things,
For then the wrong wind certainly
Would be the devil's wind, and the high trinity
Be guiltless of the windy wrongs.

But ways have changed, and most ways lead
To different places than were said
By those who planned the obvious routes
And now, mistaking the direction,
On miles of horizontal milestones,
Perplexed beyond perplexion,
Catch their poor guts.

The wind has changed, blown inside out
The coverings of dark and light,
Made meaning meaningless. The wrong wind stirs,
Puffed, old with venom, from a crusted mouth.
The changed wind blows, and there's a choice of signs
To Heaven's turned, and pious loads
Of neophytes take altered roads.

THE GOSSIPERS

The gossipers have lowered their voices,
Willing words to make the rumours certain,
Suspicious hands tug at the neighbouring vices,
Unthinking actions given causes
Stir their old bones behind cupboard and curtain.

Putting two and two together,
Informed by rumour and the register,
The virgins smelt out, three streets up,
A girl whose single bed held two
To make ends meet,
Found managers and widows wanting
In morals and full marriage bunting,
And other virgins in official fathers.

For all the inconvenience they make,
The trouble, devildom, and heartbreak,
The withered women win them bedfellows.
Nightly upon their wrinkled breasts
Press the old lies and the old ghosts.

BEFORE THE GAS FADES

Before the gas fades with a harsh last bubble,
And the hunt in the hatstand discovers no coppers,
Before the last fag and the shirt sleeves and slippers,
The century's trap will have snapped round your middle,
Before the allotment is weeded and sown,

And the oakum is picked, and the spring trees have grown green,
And the state falls to bits,
And is fed to the cats,
Before civilization rises or rots,
(It's a matter of guts,
Graft, poison, and bluff,
Sobstuff, mock reason,
The chameleon coats of the big bugs and shots,)
The jaws will have shut, and life be switched out.
Before the arrival of angel or devil,
Before evil or good, light or dark,
Before white or black, the right or left sock,
Before good or bad luck.

Man's manmade sparetime lasts the four seasons,
Is empty in springtime, and no other time lessens
The bitter, the wicked, the longlying leisure,
Sleep punctured by waking, dreams
Broken by choking,
The hunger of living, the oven and gun
That turned on and lifted in anger
Make the hunger for living
When the purse is empty
And the belly is empty,
The harder to bear and the stronger.
The century's trap will have closed for good
About you, flesh will perish, and blood
Run down the world's gutters,
Before the world steadies, stops rocking, is steady,
Or rocks, swings and rocks, before the world totters.

Caught in the trap's machinery, lights out,
With sightless eyes and hearts that do not beat,
You will not see the steadying or falling,
Under the heavy layers of the night
Not black or white or left or right.

WAS THERE A TIME

Was there a time when dancers with their fiddles
In children's circuses could stay their troubles?
There was a time they could cry over books,
But time has set its maggot on their track.
Under the arc of the sky they are unsafe.
What's never known is safest in this life.
Under the skysigns they who have no arms
Have cleanest hands, and, as the heartless ghost
Alone's unhurt, so the blind man sees best.

'WE WHO ARE YOUNG ARE OLD'

'We who are young are old. It is the oldest cry.
Age sours before youth's tasted in the mouth
And any sweetness that it has
Is sucked away.'

We who are still young are old. It is a dead cry,
The squeal of the damned out of the old pit.
We have grown weak before we could grow strong,
For us there is no shooting and no riding,
The Western man has lost one lung
And cannot mount a clotheshorse without bleeding.

Until the whisper of the last trump louden
We shall play Chopin in our summer garden,
With half-averted heads, as if to listen,
Play Patience in the parlour after dark.
For us there is no riding and no shooting,

No frosty gallops through the winter park.
We who are young sit holding yellow hands.

No faith to fix the teeth on carries
Men old before their time into dark valleys
Where death lies dead asleep, one bright eye open,
No faith to sharpen the old wits leaves us
Lost in the shades, no course, no use
To fight through the invisible weeds,
No faith to follow is the world's curse
That falls on chaos.

There is but one message for the earth,
Young men with fallen chests and old men's breath,
Women with cancer at their sides
And cancerous speaking dripping from their mouths,
And lovers turning on the gas,
Ex-soldiers with horrors for a face,
A pig's snout for a nose,
The lost in doubt, the nearly mad, the young
Who, undeserving, have suffered the earth's wrong,
The living dead left over from the war,
The living after, the filled with fear,
The caught in the cage, the broken winged,
The flying loose, albino eyed, wing singed,
The white, the black, the yellow and mulatto
From Harlem, Bedlam, Babel, and the Ghetto,
The Piccadilly men, the back street drunks,
The grafters of cats' heads on chickens' trunks,
The whole, the crippled, the weak and strong,
The Western man with one lung gone—
Faith fixed beyond the spinning stars,
Fixed faith, believing and worshipping together
In god or gods, christ or his father,
Mary, virgin, or any other.
Faith. Faith. Firm faith in many or one,

Faith fixed like a star beyond the stars,
And the skysigns and the night lights,
And the shores of the last sun.

We who are young are old, and unbelieving,
Sit at our hearths from morning until evening,
Warming dry hands and listening to the wind.
We have no faith to set between our teeth.
Believe, believe and be saved, we cry, who have no faith.

OUT OF A WAR OF WITS

Out of a war of wits, when folly of words
Was the world's to me, and syllables
Fell hard as whips on an old wound,
My brain came crying into the fresh light,
Called for confessor but there was none
To purge after the wits' fight,
And I was struck dumb by the sun.
Praise that my body be whole, I've limbs,
Not stumps, after the hour of battle,
For the body's brittle and the skin's white.
Praise that only the wits are hurt after the wits' fight.
Overwhelmed by the sun, with a torn brain
I stand beneath the clouds' confessional,
But the hot beams rob me of speech,
After the perils of friends' talk
Reach asking arms up to the milky sky,
After a volley of questions and replies
Lift wit-hurt head for sun to sympathize,
And the sun heals, closing sore eyes.
It is good that the sun shine,
And, after it has sunk, the sane moon,

For out of a house of matchboard and stone
Where men would argue till the stars be green,
It is good to step onto the earth, alone,
And be struck dumb, if only for a time.

42

THEIR FACES SHONE UNDER SOME RADIANCE

Their faces shone under some radiance
Of mingled moonlight and lamplight
That turned the empty kisses into meaning,
The island of such penny love
Into a costly country, the graves
That neighboured them to wells of warmth,
(And skeletons had sap). One minute
Their faces shone; the midnight rain
Hung pointed in the wind,
Before the moon shifted and the sap ran out,
She, in her cheap frock, saying some cheap thing,
And he replying,
Not knowing radiance came and passed.
The suicides parade again, now ripe for dying.

43

I HAVE LONGED TO MOVE AWAY

I have longed to move away
From the hissing of the spent lie
And the old terrors' continual cry
Growing more terrible as the day
Goes over the hill into the deep sea;
I have longed to move away
From the repetition of salutes,
For there are ghosts in the air

And ghostly echoes on paper,
And the thunder of calls and notes.

I have longed to move away but am afraid;
Some life, yet unspent, might explode
Out of the old lie burning on the ground,
And, crackling into the air, leave me half-blind.
Neither by night's ancient fear,
The parting of hat from hair,
Pursed lips at the receiver,
Shall I fall to death's feather.
By these I would not care to die,
Half convention and half lie.

44

TO FOLLOW THE FOX

To follow the fox at the hounds' tails
And at their baying move a tailor's inch
To follow, wild as the chicken stealer,
Scent through the clutches of the heather,
Leads to fool's paradise where the redcoated killer
Deserves no brush, but a fool's ambush.
Following the nose down dell, up rise
Into the map-backed hills where paths
Cross all directions, bracken points to the skies,
Leads, too, to a lead pit, whinny and fall,
No fox, no good, fool's, not a fox's, hole,
And that is the reward of labour
Through heath and heather at the mind's will.
To follow the nose if the nose goes
Wisely at the dogs' tails, leads
Through easier heather to the foul lair
Over a road thick with the bones of words.
If hunting means anything more than the chase

On a mare's back of a mare's nest or a goose,
Then only over corpses shall the feet tread,
Crunching the already broken,
And this way leads to good and bad,
Where more than snails are friends.

45

THE PLOUGHMAN'S GONE

The ploughman's gone, the hansom driver,
Left in the records of living a not-to-be-broken picture,
In sun and rain working for good and gain,
Left only the voice in the old village choir
To remember, cast stricture on mechanics and man.
The windmills of the world still stand
With wooden arms revolving in the wind
Against the rusty sword and the old horse
Bony and spavined, rich with fleas.
But the horses are gone and the reins are green
As the hands that held them in my father's time.
The wireless snarls on the hearth.
No more toils over the fields
The rawboned horse to a man's voice
Telling it this, patting its black nose:
You shall go as the others have gone,
Lay your head on a hard bed of stone,
And have the raven for companion.
The ploughman's gone, the hansom driver,
With rain-beaten hands holding the whip,
Masters over unmastered nature,
Streets' stock, of the moon lit, ill lit, field and town,
Lie cold, with their horses, for raven and kite.

Man toils now on an iron saddle, riding
In sun and rain over the dry shires,

[45]

Hearing the engines, and the wheat dying.
Sometimes at his ear the engine's voice
Revolves over and over again
The same tune as in my father's time:
You shall go as the others have gone,
Lay your head on a hard bed of stone,
And have the raven for companion.
It is the engine and not the raven.
Man who once drove is driven in sun and rain.
It is the engine for companion.
It is the engine under the unaltered sun.

46

POET: 1935

See, on gravel paths under the harpstrung trees
He steps so near the water that a swan's wing
Might play upon his lank locks with its wind,
The lake's voice and the rolling of mock waves
Make discord with the voice within his ribs
That thunders as heart thunders, slows as heart slows.
Is not his heart imprisoned by the summer
Snaring the whistles of the birds
And fastening in its cage the flowers' colour?
No, he's a stranger, outside the season's humour,
Moves, among men caught by the sun,
With heart unlocked upon the gigantic earth.
He alone is free, and, free, moans to the sky.
He, too, could touch the season's lips and smile,
Under the hanging branches hear the winds' harps.
But he is left. Summer to him
Is the unbosoming of the sun.

So shall he step till summer loosens its hold
On the canvas sky, and all hot colours melt

Into the browns of autumn and the sharp whites of winter,
And so complain, in a vain voice, to the stars.

Even among his own kin is he lost,
Is love a shadow on the wall,
Among all living men is a sad ghost.
He is not man's nor woman's man,
Leper among a clean people
Walks with the hills for company,
And has the mad trees' talk by heart.

An image of decay disturbs the crocus
Opening its iris mouth upon the sill
Where fifty flowers breed in a fruit box,
And washing water spilt upon their necks
Cools any ardour they may have
And he destroys, though flowers are his loves,
If love he can being no woman's man.
An image born out of the uproarious spring
Hastens the time of the geranium to breathe;
Life, till the change of mood, forks
From the unwatered leaves and the stiff stalks,
The old flowers' legs too taut to dance,
But he makes them dance, cut capers
Choreographed on paper.
The image changes, and the flowers drop
Into their prison with a slack sound,
Fresh images surround the tremendous moon,
Or catch all death that's in the air.

O lonely among many, the gods' man,
Knowing exceeding grief and the gods' sorrow
That, like a razor, skims, cuts, and turns,
Aches till the metal meets the marrow,
You, too, know the exceeding joy

And the triumphant crow of laughter.
Out of a bird's wing writing on a cloud
You capture more than man or woman guesses;
Rarer delight shoots in the blood
At the deft movements of the irises
Growing in public places than man knows.

See, on gravel paths under the harpstrung trees,
Feeling the summer wind, hearing the swans,
Leaning from windows over a length of lawns,
On tumbling hills admiring the sea,
I am alone, alone complain to the stars.
Who are his friends? The wind is his friend,
The glow-worm lights his darkness, and
The snail tells of coming rain.

47

LIGHT, I KNOW, TREADS THE TEN MILLION STARS

Light, I know, treads the ten million stars,
And blooms in the Hesperides. Light stirs
Out of the heavenly sea onto the moon's shores.
Such light shall not illuminate my fears
And catch a turnip ghost in every cranny.
I have been frightened of the dark for years.
When the sun falls and the moon stares,
My heart hurls from my side and tears
Drip from my open eyes as honey
Drips from the humming darkness of the hive.
I am a timid child when light is dead.
Unless I learn the night I shall go mad.
It is night's terrors I must learn to love,
Or pray for day to some attentive god
Who on his cloud hears all my wishes,

Hears and refuses.
Light walks the sky, leaving no print,
And there is always day, the shining of some sun,
In those high globes I cannot count,
And some shine for a second and are gone,
Leaving no print.
But lunar light will not glow in my blackness,
Make bright its corners where a skeleton
Sits back and smiles, a tiny corpse
Turns to the roof a hideous grimace,
Or mice play with an ivory tooth.
Stars' light and sun's light will not shine
As clearly as the light of my own brain,
Will only dim life, and light death.
I must learn night's light or go mad.

48

AND DEATH SHALL HAVE NO DOMINION

And death shall have no dominion.
Dead men naked they shall be one
With the man in the wind and the west moon;
When their bones are picked clean and the clean bones gone,
They shall have stars at elbow and foot;
Though they go mad they shall be sane,
Though they sink through the sea they shall rise again;
Though lovers be lost love shall not;
And death shall have no dominion.

And death shall have no dominion.
Under the windings of the sea
They lying long shall not die windily;
Twisting on racks when sinews give way,
Strapped to a wheel, yet they shall not break;

Faith in their hands shall snap in two,
And the unicorn evils run them through;
Split all ends up they shan't crack;
And death shall have no dominion.

And death shall have no dominion.
No more may gulls cry at their ears
Or waves break loud on the seashores;
Where blew a flower may a flower no more
Lift its head to the blows of the rain;
Though they be mad and dead as nails,
Heads of the characters hammer through daisies;
Break in the sun till the sun breaks down,
And death shall have no dominion.

49

OUT OF THE PIT

Within his head revolved a little world
Where wheels, confusing music, confused doubts,
Rolled down all images into the pits
Where half dead vanities were sleeping curled
Like cats, and lusts lay half hot in the cold.

Within his head the engines made their hell,
The veins at either temple whipped him mad,
And, mad, he called his curses upon God,
Spied moon-mad beasts carousing on the hill,
Mad birds in trees, and mad fish in a pool.
Across the sun was spread a crazy smile.
The moon leered down the valley like a fool.

Now did the softest sound of foot or voice
Echo a hundred times, the flight of birds

Drum harshly on the air, the lightning swords
Tear with a great sound through the skies,
And there was thunder in an opening rose.

All reason broke, and horror walked the roads.
A smile let loose a devil, a bell struck.
He could hear women breathing in the dark,
See women's faces under living snoods,
With serpents' mouths and scalecophidian voids
Where eyes should be, and nostrils full of toads.

Taxis and lilies to tinned music stepped
A measure on the lawn where cupids blew
Water from nose and arse, a Sanger's show
Paraded up the aisles and in the crypt
Of churches made from abstract and concrete.
Pole-sitting girls descended for a meal,
Stopped non-stop dancing to let hot feet cool,
Or all-in wrestling for torn limbs to heal,
The moon leered down the valley like a fool.

Where, what's my God among this crazy rattling
Of knives on forks, he cried, of nerve on nerve,
Man's rib on woman's, straight line on a curve,
And hand to buttock, man to engine, battling,
Bruising, where's God's my Shepherd, God is Love?
No loving shepherd in this upside life.

So crying, he was dragged into the sewer,
Voles at his armpits, down the sad canal
Where floated a dead dog who made him ill,
Plunged in black waters, under hail and fire,
Knee-deep in vomit. I saw him there,
And thus I saw him searching for his soul.

And swimming down the gutters he looks up
At cotton worlds revolving on a hip,

Riding on girders of the air, looks down
On garages and clinics in the town.

Where, what's my God among this taxi stepping,
This lily crawling round the local pubs?
It was November there were whizzbangs hopping,
But now there are the butt-ends of spent squibs.

So crying, he was pushed into the Jordan.
He, too, has known the agony in the Garden,
And felt a skewer enter at his side.
He, too, has seen the world as bottom rotten,
Kicked, with a clatter, ash-bins marked verboten,
And heard the teeth of weasels drawing blood.

And thus I saw him. He was poised like this,
One hand at head, the other at a loss,
Between the street-lamps and the ill-lit sky,
And thus, between the seasons, heard him cry:

Where, what's my God? I have been mad, am mad,
Have searched for shells and signs on the sea shore,
Stuck straw and seven stars upon my hair,
And leant on stiles and on the golden bar,
I have ridden on gutter dung and cloud.
Under a hideous sea where coral men
Feed in the armpits of drowned girls, I've swum
And sunk; waved flags to every fife and drum;
Said all the usual things over and again;
Lain with parched things; loved dogs and women;
I have desired the circle of the sun.
Tested by fire, double thumb to nose,
I've mocked the moving of the universe.

Where, what? There was commotion in the skies,
But no god rose. I have seen bad and worse,

Gibed the coitus of the stars. No god
Comes from my evil or my good. Mad, mad,
Feeling the pinpricks of the blood, I've said
The novel things. But it has been no good.

Crying such words, he left the crying crowds,
Unshackled the weights of words from tired limbs,
And took to feeding birds with broken crumbs
Of old divinities, split bits of names.
Very alone, he ploughed the only way.
And thus I saw him in a square of fields,
Knocking off turnip tops, with trees for friends,
And thus, some time later, I heard him say:

Out of the buildings of the day I've stepped
To hermits' huts, and talked to ancient men.
Out of the noise into quiet I ran.
My God's a shepherd, God's the love I hoped.
The moon peers down the valley like a saint.
Taxis and lilies, noise and no noise,
Pair off, make harmonies, a harmonious chord,
For he has found his soul in loneliness,
Now he is one with many, one with all,
Fire and Jordan and the sad canal.
Now he has heard and read the happy word.
Still, in his hut, he broods among his birds.
I see him in the crowds, not shut
From you or me or wind or rat
Or this or that.

WE LYING BY SEASAND

We lying by seasand, watching yellow
And the grave sea, mock who deride
Who follow the red rivers, hollow
Alcove of words out of cicada shade,
For in this yellow grave of sand and sea
A calling for colour calls with the wind
That's grave and gay as grave and sea
Sleeping on either hand.
The lunar silences, the silent tide
Lapping the still canals, the dry tide-master
Ribbed between desert and water storm,
Should cure our ills of the water
With a one-coloured calm;
The heavenly music over the sand
Sounds with the grains as they hurry
Hiding the golden mountains and mansions
Of the grave, gay, seaside land.
Bound by a sovereign strip, we lie,
Watch yellow, wish for wind to blow away
The strata of the shore and drown red rock;
But wishes breed not, neither
Can we fend off rock arrival,
Lie watching yellow until the golden weather
Breaks, O my heart's blood, like a heart and hill.

NO MAN BELIEVES

No man believes who, when a star falls shot,
Cries not aloud blind as a bat,
Cries not in terror when a bird is drawn

Into the quicksand feathers down,
Who does not make a wound in faith
When any light goes out, and life is death.

No man believes who cries not, God is not,
Who feels not coldness in the heat,
In the breasted summer longs not for spring,
No breasted girl, no man who, young
And green, sneers not at the old sky.
No man believes who does not wonder why.

Believe and be saved. No man believes
Who curses not what makes and saves,
No man upon this cyst of earth
Believes who does not lance his faith,
No man, no man, no man.

And this is true, no man can live
Who does not bury God in a deep grave
And then raise up the skeleton again,
No man who does not break and make,
Who in the bones finds not new faith,
Lends not flesh to ribs and neck,
Who does not break and make his final faith.

52

WHY EAST WIND CHILLS

Why east wind chills and south wind cools
Shall not be known till windwell dries
And west's no longer drowned
In winds that bring the fruit and rind
Of many a hundred falls;
Why silk is soft and the stone wounds

The child shall question all his days,
Why night-time rain and the breast's blood
Both quench his thirst he'll have a black reply.

When cometh Jack Frost? the children ask.
Shall they clasp a comet in their fists?
Not till, from high and low, their dust
Sprinkles in children's eyes a long-last sleep
And dusk is crowded with the children's ghosts,
Shall a white answer echo from the rooftops.

All things are known: the stars' advice
Calls some content to travel with the winds,
Though what the stars ask as they round
Time upon time the towers of the skies
Is heard but little till the stars go out.
I hear content, and 'Be content'
Ring like a handbell through the corridors,
And 'Know no answer', and I know
No answer to the children's cry
Of echo's answer and the man of frost
And ghostly comets over the raised fists.

53

GREEK PLAY IN A GARDEN

A woman wails her dead among the trees,
Under the green roof grieves the living;
The living sun laments the dying skies,
Lamenting falls. Pity Electra's loving

Of all Orestes' continent of pride
Dust in the little country of an urn,
Of Agamemnon and his kingly blood
That cries along her veins. No sun or moon

[56]

Shall lamp the raven darkness of her face,
And no Aegean wind cool her cracked heart;
There are no seacaves deeper than her eyes;
Day treads the trees and she the cavernous night.

Among the trees the language of the dead
Sounds, rich with life, out of a painted mask;
The queen is slain; Orestes' hands drip blood;
And women talk of horror to the dusk.

There can be few tears left: Electra wept
A country's tears and voiced a world's despair
At flesh that perishes and blood that's spilt
And love that goes down like a flower.

Pity the living who are lost, alone;
The dead in Hades have their host of friends,
The dead queen walketh with Mycenae's king
Through Hades' groves and the Eternal Lands.

Pity Electra loveless, she whose grief
Drowns and is drowned, who utters to the stars
Her syllables, and to the gods her love;
Pity the poor unpitied who are strange with tears.

Among the garden trees a pigeon calls,
And knows no woe that these sad players mouth
Of evil oracles and funeral ills;
A pigeon calls and women talk of death.

54

PRAISE TO THE ARCHITECTS

Praise to the architects;
Dramatic shadows in a tin box;
Nonstop; stoppress; vinegar from wisecracks;

Praise to the architects;
Radio's a building in the air;
The poster is today's text,
The message comes from negro mystics,
An old chatterbox, barenaveled at Nice,
Who steps on the gas;
Praise to the architects;
A pome's a building on a page;
Keatings is good for lice,
A pinch of Auden is the lion's feast;
Praise to the architects;
Empty, To Let, are signs on this new house;
To leave it empty's lion's or louse's choice;
Lion or louse? Take your own advice;
Praise to the architects.

55

HERE IN THIS SPRING

Here in this spring, stars float along the void;
Here in this ornamental winter
Down pelts the naked weather;
This summer buries a spring bird.

Symbols are selected from the years'
Slow rounding of four seasons' coasts,
In autumn teach three seasons' fires
And four birds' notes.

I should tell summer from the trees, the worms
Tell, if at all, the winter's storms
Or the funeral of the sun;
I should learn spring by the cuckooing,
And the slug should teach me destruction.

A worm tells summer better than the clock,
The slug's a living calendar of days;
What shall it tell me if a timeless insect
Says the world wears away?

WE HAVE THE FAIRY TALES BY HEART

We have the fairy tales by heart,
No longer tremble at a bishop's hat,
And the thunder's first note;
We have these little things off pat,
Avoid church as a rat;
We scorn the juggernaut,
And the great wheels' rut;
Half of the old gang's shot,
Thank God, but the enemy stays put.

We know our Mother Goose and Eden,
No longer fear the walker in the garden,
And the fibs for children;
The old spells are undone.
But still ghosts madden,
A cupboard skeleton
Raises the hairs of lad and maiden.

If dead men walked they, too, would holler
At sight of death, the last two fisted killer
Stained a blood colour;
A panic's pallor
Would turn the dead yellow.

We have by heart the children's stories,
Have blown sky high the nursery of fairies;

Still a world of furies
Burns in many mirrors.

Death and evil are twin spectres.
What shall destruction count if these are fixtures?
Why blot the pictures
Of elves and satyrs
If these two gnomes remain unmoved by strictures?

We have the stories backwards,
Torn out magic from the hearts of cowards
By nape and gizzards;
There are two laggards,
Death and evil, too slow in heeding words.

Tear by the roots these twin growths in your gut;
Shall we learn fairy tales off pat,
Not benefit from that?
Burn out the lasting rot,
Fear death as little as the thunder's shot,
The holy hat.

57

'FIND MEAT ON BONES'

'Find meat on bones that soon have none,
And drink in the two milked crags,
The merriest marrow and the dregs
Before the ladies' breasts are hags
And the limbs are torn.
Disturb no winding-sheets, my son,
But when the ladies are cold as stone
Then hang a ram rose over the rags.

'Rebel against the binding moon
And the parliament of sky,
The kingcrafts of the wicked sea,
Autocracy of night and day,
Dictatorship of sun.
Rebel against the flesh and bone,
The word of the blood, the wily skin,
And the maggot no man can slay.'

'The thirst is quenched, the hunger gone,
And my heart is cracked across;
My face is haggard in the glass,
My lips are withered with a kiss,
My breasts are thin.
A merry girl took me for man,
I laid her down and told her sin,
And put beside her a ram rose.

'The maggot that no man can kill
And the man no rope can hang
Rebel against my father's dream
That out of a bower of red swine
Howls the foul fiend to heel.
I cannot murder, like a fool,
Season and sunshine, grace and girl,
Nor can I smother the sweet waking.'

Black night still ministers the moon,
And the sky lays down her laws,
The sea speaks in a kingly voice,
Light and dark are no enemies
But one companion.
'War on the spider and the wren!
War on the destiny of man!
Doom on the sun!'
Before death takes you, O take back this.

[61]

EARS IN THE TURRETS HEAR

Ears in the turrets hear
Hands grumble on the door,
Eyes in the gables see
The fingers at the locks.
Shall I unbolt or stay
Alone till the day I die
Unseen by stranger-eyes
In this white house?
Hands, hold you poison or grapes?

Beyond this island bound
By a thin sea of flesh
And a bone coast,
The land lies out of sound
And the hills out of mind.
No birds or flying fish
Disturbs this island's rest.

Ears in this island hear
The wind pass like a fire,
Eyes in this island see
Ships anchor off the bay.
Shall I run to the ships
With the wind in my hair,
Or stay till the day I die
And welcome no sailor?
Ships, hold you poison or grapes?

Hands grumble on the door,
Ships anchor off the bay,
Rain beats the sand and slates.

Shall I let in the stranger,
Shall I welcome the sailor,
Or stay till the day I die?

Hands of the stranger and holds of the ships,
Hold you poison or grapes?

59
THE WOMAN SPEAKS

The Woman Speaks:
    No food suffices but the food of death;
    Sweet is the waxen blood, honey the falling flesh;
    There is no fountain springing from the earth
    Cool as the wax-red fountains of the veins;
    No cradle's warmer than this perished breast,
    And hid behind the fortress of the ribs
    The heart lies ready for the raven's mouth,
    And lustreless within the ruined face
    The eyes remark the antics of the hawk.

    The sniper laid him low and strewed his brains;
    One would not think the greenness of this valley

    Could in a day be sick with so much blood;
    What were young limbs are faggots on the land,
    And young guts dry beneath the sickened sun.
    Let me not think, O God of carnage,
    Of ravens at the hero's meat and nerves
    Pecking and nestling all the time of night.

    The grass he covers is a pretty green;
    He has the still moon and the hundred stars;
    He learns the carrion pickers of the sky,
    And on his shoulders fall their world of wings,
    And on his ears hosannas of the grave.

His narrow house is walled with blades of grass,
Roofed with the sky and patterned with blond bones;
The birds make him his cerements of plumes,
Cerecloth of weed, and build an ordured bed.

Since the first flesh of man was riven
By scalpel lightning from the rifted sky,
Man's marrow barbed, and breast ripped with a steel,
All that was loved and loved made the fowls' food,
Grief, like an open wound, has cried to heaven.
No food suffices but the food of death;
Death's appetite is sharpened by the bullet's thumb;
Yet he is dead, and still by woman's womb
Hungers for quickening, and my lonely lips
Hunger for him who dungs the valley fields.

There shall be no mute mourning over his acre,
Sorrow shall have no words, no willow wearing;
Rain shall defile and cover, wind bear away
The saddest dust in all this hollow world.

Old men whose blood is hindered in their veins,
Whom cancer crops, whose drinking rusts, these die;
These die who shovel the last home of man;
The sniper dies; the fingers from the sky
Strangle the little children in their beds;
One day my woman's body will be cold.

So I have come to know, but knowledge aches;
I know that age is snow upon the hair,
Wind carven lines around the drooping mouth;
And raven youth will feast but where he will.

Since the first womb spat forth a baby's corpse,
The mother's cry has fumed about the winds;

O tidal winds, cast up her cry for me;
That I may drown, let loose her flood of tears.

It was a haggard night the first flesh died,
And shafted hawks came snarling down the sky;
A mouse it was played with an ivory tooth,
And ravens fed confection to their young.

Palm of the earth, O sprinkle on my head
That dust you hold, O strew that little left;
Let what remains of that first miracle
Be sour in my hair. That I may learn
The mortal miracle, let that first dust
Tell me of him who feeds the raging birds.

60

SHALL GODS BE SAID TO THUMP THE CLOUDS

Shall gods be said to thump the clouds
When clouds are cursed by thunder,
Be said to weep when weather howls?
Shall rainbows be their tunics' colour?

When it is rain where are the gods?
Shall it be said they sprinkle water
From garden cans, or free the floods?

Shall it be said that, venuswise,
An old god's dugs are pressed and pricked,
The wet night scolds me like a nurse?

It shall be said that gods are stone.
Shall a dropped stone drum on the ground,

Flung gravel chime? Let the stones speak
With tongues that talk all tongues.

61

THE HAND THAT SIGNED THE PAPER

The hand that signed the paper felled a city;
Five sovereign fingers taxed the breath,
Doubled the globe of dead and halved a country;
These five kings did a king to death.

The mighty hand leads to a sloping shoulder,
The finger joints are cramped with chalk;
A goose's quill has put an end to murder
That put an end to talk.

The hand that signed the treaty bred a fever,
And famine grew, and locusts came;
Great is the hand that holds dominion over
Man by a scribbled name.

The five kings count the dead but do not soften
The crusted wound nor stroke the brow;
A hand rules pity as a hand rules heaven;
Hands have no tears to flow.

62

LET FOR ONE MOMENT A FAITH STATEMENT

Let for one moment a faith statement
Rule the blank sheet of sleep,
The virgin lines be mated with a circle.

[66]

A circle spins. Let each revolving spoke
Turn and churn nightseed till it curdle.

Let for one moment a faith statement
Strip the dreams' livery,
And gods be changed as often as the shift.
God is the same though he be praised as many,
Remains though gods be felled till none are left.

Let for one moment a faith statement
See the first living light,
And your maieutic slumber drag it forth.
The child tells, when the trembling chord is cut,
God shall be gods and many deaths be death.

63

YOU ARE THE RULER OF THIS REALM OF FLESH

You are the ruler of this realm of flesh,
And this hill of bone and hair
Moves to the Mahomet of your hand.
But all this land gives off a charnel stench,
The wind smacks of the poor
Dumb dead the crannies house and hide.

You rule the thudding heart that bites the side;
The heart steps to death's finger,
The brain acts to the legal dead.
Why should I think on death when you are ruler?

You are my flesh's ruler whom I treason,
Housing death in your kingdom,
Paying heed to the thirsty voice.

Condemn me to an everlasting facing
Of the dead eyes of children
And their rivers of blood turned to ice.

BEFORE I KNOCKED

Before I knocked and flesh let enter,
With liquid hands tapped on the womb,
I who was shapeless as the water
That shaped the Jordan near my home
Was brother to Mnetha's daughter
And sister to the fathering worm.

I who was deaf to spring and summer,
Who knew not sun nor moon by name,
Felt thud beneath my flesh's armour,
As yet was in a molten form,
The leaden stars, the rainy hammer
Swung by my father from his dome.

I knew the message of the winter,
The darted hail, the childish snow,
And the wind was my sister suitor;
Wind in me leaped, the hellborn dew;
My veins flowed with the Eastern weather;
Ungotten I knew night and day.

As yet ungotten, I did suffer;
The rack of dreams my lily bones
Did twist into a living cipher,
And flesh was snipped to cross the lines
Of gallow crosses on the liver
And brambles in the wringing brains.

My throat knew thirst before the structure
Of skin and vein around the well
Where words and water make a mixture
Unfailing till the blood runs foul;
My heart knew love, my belly hunger;
I smelt the maggot in my stool.

And time cast forth my mortal creature
To drift or drown upon the seas
Acquainted with the salt adventure
Of tides that never touch the shores.
I who was rich was made the richer
By sipping at the vine of days.

I, born of flesh and ghost, was neither
A ghost nor man, but mortal ghost.
And I was struck down by death's feather.
I was a mortal to the last
Long breath that carried to my father
The message of his dying christ.

You who bow down at cross and altar,
Remember me and pity Him
Who took my flesh and bone for armour
And doublecrossed my mother's womb.

65

WE SEE RISE THE SECRET WIND

We see rise the secret wind behind the brain,
The sphinx of light sit on the eyes,
The code of stars translate in heaven.
A secret night descends between
The skull, the cells, the cabinned ears
Holding for ever the dead moon.

A shout went up to heaven like a rocket,
Woe from the rabble of the blind
Adorners of the city's forehead,
Gilders of streets, the rabble hand
Saluting the busy brotherhood
Of rod and wheel that wake the dead.

A city godhead, turbine moved, steel sculptured,
Glitters in the electric streets;
A city saviour, in the orchard
Of lamp-posts and high-volted fruits,
Speaks a steel gospel to the wretched
Wheel-winders and fixers of bolts.

We hear rise the secret wind behind the brain,
The secret voice cry in our ears,
The city gospel shout to heaven.
Over the electric godhead grows
One God, more mighty than the sun.
The cities have not robbed our eyes.

66

TAKE THE NEEDLES AND THE KNIVES

Take the needles and the knives,
Put an iron at the eyes,
Let a maggot at the ear
Toil away till music dies.

Let me in the devil's groves
Cut my fingers on a rose,
Let the maggot of despair
Drain the spring where promise goes.

[70]

Take the scissors and the pan,
Let the tiny armies lap,
And the heralds of decay,
At the labyrinthine pap.

Choke the bladder with a stone,
Fill the veins the fevers broke,
All the cabinned faiths deny
And the feeble house of hope.

And a child might be my slayer,
And a mother in her labour
Murder with a cry of pain;
Half a smile might be her sabre.

Let it be a sword of fire,
Lightning or the darting viper,
Thunder's rod or man's machine;
God and I will pay the sniper.

Flesh is suffered, is laid low,
Mixes, ripens, in the loam;
Spirit suffers but is still
In its labyrinthine home.

In the wilderness they go,
Flesh and spirit, babe and dam,
Walking in the evening's cool
With the leper and the lamb.

In the darkness dam and babe
Tremble at the starry stain,
And the ruin of the sky;
Darkness is the dam of pain.

Take the scissors to this globe,
Firmament of flesh and bone
Lawed and ordered from on high
By a godhead of my own.

Mother root that shot me forth,
Like a green tree through the sward,
Mothers me until I die,
And my father was the lord.

When I yield the tree to death,
In the country of the dead
Dam and sire, living, lo,
Will be breathing by my bed.

Take the needles to this tree
Bowing on its mossy knees,
Stitch the stem on to the leaf,
Let the sap leak in the breeze.

Thread and torture all the day;
You but wound the lord of days;
Slay me, slay the god of love;
God is slain in many ways.

Question: Shall the root be true
And the green tree trust the root?
Answer: Shall a mother lie
In the face of seed and fruit?

Question: When shall root-dam die?
Answer: When her babe denies her.
Question: When shall root-dam grow?
Answer: When the green leaves prize her.

NOT FOREVER SHALL THE LORD OF THE RED HAIL

Not forever shall the Lord of the red hail
Hold in his velvet hand the can of blood;
He shall be wise and let his brimstone spill,
Free from their burning nests the arrows' brood.
And sweet shall fall contagion from his side,
And loud his anger stamp upon the hill.

As fire falls, two hemispheres divide,
Shall drown the boys of battle in their swill,
The stock and steel that bayonet from the mud,
The fields yet undivided behind the skull.
Both mind and matter at the scalding word
Shall fall away, and leave one singing shell.

A hole in space shall keep the shape of thought,
The lines of earth, the curving of the heart,
And from this darkness spin the golden soul.
Intangible my world shall come to naught,
The solid world shall wither in the heat,
How soon, how soon, O lord of the red hail!

BEFORE WE MOTHERNAKED FALL

Before we mothernaked fall
Upon the land of gold or oil,
Between the raid and the response
Of flesh and bones,
Our claim is staked for once and all

Near to the quarry or the well,
Before the promises fulfill
And joys are pains.

Then take the gusher or the field
Where all the hidden stones are gold,
We have no choice, the choice was made
Before our blood;
And I will build my liquid world,
And you, before the breath is cold
And veins are spilled and doom is turned,
Your solid land.

69

THE SUN BURNS THE MORNING

The sun burns the morning, a bush in the brain;
Moon walks the river and raises the dead;
Here in my wilderness wanders the blood;
And the sweat on the brow makes a sign,
And the wailing heart's nailed to the side.

Here is a universe bred in the bone,
Here is a saviour who sings like a bird,
Here the night shelters and here the stars shine,
Here a mild baby speaks his first word
In the stable under the skin.

Under the ribs sail the moon and the sun;
A cross is tatooed on the breast of the child,
And sewn on his skull a scarlet thorn;
A mother in labour pays twice her pain,
Once for the Virgin's child, once for her own.

MY HERO BARES HIS NERVES

My hero bares his nerves along my wrist
That rules from wrist to shoulder,
Unpacks the head that, like a sleepy ghost,
Leans on my mortal ruler,
The proud spine spurning turn and twist.

And these poor nerves so wired to the skull
Ache on the lovelorn paper
I hug to love with my unruly scrawl
That utters all love hunger
And tells the page the empty ill.

My hero bares my side and sees his heart
Tread, like a naked Venus,
The beach of flesh, and wind her bloodred plait;
Stripping my loin of promise,
He promises a secret heat.

He holds the wire from this box of nerves
Praising the mortal error
Of birth and death, the two sad knaves of thieves,
And the hunger's emperor;
He pulls the chain, the cistern moves.

SONG

Love me, not as the dreaming nurses
My falling lungs, nor as the cypress
In his age the lass's clay.
Love me and lift your mask.

Love me, not as the girls of heaven
Their airy lovers, nor the mermaiden
Her salty lovers in the sea.
Love me and lift your mask.

Love me, not as the ruffling pigeon
The tops of trees, nor as the legion
Of the gulls the lip of waves.
Love me and lift your mask.

Love me, as loves the mole his darkness
And the timid deer the tigress:
Hate and fear be your two loves.
Love me and lift your mask.

72

THROUGH THESE LASHED RINGS

Through these lashed rings set deep inside their hollows
I eye the ring of earth, the airy circle,
My Maker's flesh that garments my clayfellows.
And through these trembling rings set in their valley
Whereon the hooded hair casts down its girdle,
A holy voice acquaints me with His glory.

Through, I tell you, your two midnight lips I pray
To that unending sea around my island
The water-spirit moves as it is hidden,
And with not one fear-beggared syllable
Praise Him who springs and fills the tidal well.

And through these eyes God marks myself revolving,
And from these tongue-plucked senses draws His tune;
Inside this mouth I feel His message moving

Acquainting me with my divinity;
And through these ears He harks my fire burn
His awkward heart into some symmetry.

73

THE FORCE THAT THROUGH THE GREEN FUSE
DRIVES THE FLOWER

The force that through the green fuse drives the flower
Drives my green age; that blasts the roots of trees
Is my destroyer.
And I am dumb to tell the crooked rose
My youth is bent by the same wintry fever.

The force that drives the water through the rocks
Drives my red blood; that dries the mouthing streams
Turns mine to wax.
And I am dumb to mouth unto my veins
How at the mountain spring the same mouth sucks.

The hand that whirls the water in the pool
Stirs the quicksand; that ropes the blowing wind
Hauls my shroud sail.
And I am dumb to tell the hanging man
How of my clay is made the hangman's lime.

The lips of time leech to the fountain head;
Love drips and gathers, but the fallen blood
Shall calm her sores.
And I am dumb to tell a weather's wind
How time has ticked a heaven round the stars.

And I am dumb to tell the lover's tomb
How at my sheet goes the same crooked worm.

FROM LOVE'S FIRST FEVER TO HER PLAGUE

From love's first fever to her plague, from the soft second
And to the hollow minute of the womb,
From the unfolding to the scissored caul,
The time for breast and the green apron age
When no mouth stirred about the hanging famine,
All world was one, one windy nothing,
My world was christened in a stream of milk.
And earth and sky were as one airy hill,
The sun and moon shed one white light.

From the first print of the unshodden foot, the lifting
Hand, the breaking of the hair,
From the first secret of the heart, the warning ghost,
And to the first dumb wonder at the flesh,
The sun was red, the moon was grey,
The earth and sky were as two mountains meeting.

The body prospered, teeth in the marrowed gums,
The growing bones, the rumour of manseed
Within the hallowed gland, blood blessed the heart,
And the four winds, that had long blown as one,
Shone in my ears the light of sound,
Called in my eyes the sound of light.
And yellow was the multiplying sand,
Each golden grain spat life into its fellow,
Green was the singing house.

The plum my mother picked matured slowly,
The boy she dropped from darkness at her side
Into the sided lap of light grew strong,
Was muscled, matted, wise to the crying thigh

And to the voice that, like a voice of hunger,
Itched in the noise of wind and sun.

And from the first declension of the flesh
I learnt man's tongue, to twist the shapes of thoughts
Into the stony idiom of the brain,
To shade and knit anew the patch of words
Left by the dead who, in their moonless acre,
Need no word's warmth.
The root of tongues ends in a spentout cancer,
That but a name, where maggots have their X.

I learnt the verbs of will, and had my secret;
The code of night tapped on my tongue;
What had been one was many sounding minded.

One womb, one mind, spewed out the matter,
One breast gave suck the fever's issue;
From the divorcing sky I learnt the double,
The two-framed globe that spun into a score;
A million minds gave suck to such a bud
As forks my eye;
Youth did condense; the tears of spring
Dissolved in summer and the hundred seasons;
One sun, one manna, warmed and fed.

75

THE ALMANAC OF TIME

The almanac of time hangs in the brain;
The seasons numbered by the inward sun,
The winter years, move in the pit of man;

His graph is measured as the page of pain
Shifts to the redwombed pen.

The calendar of age hangs in the heart,
A lover's thought tears down the dated sheet,
The inch of time's protracted to a foot
By youth and age, the mortal state and thought
Ageing both day and night.

The word of time lies on the chaptered bone,
The seed of time is sheltered in the loin:
The grains of life must seethe beneath the sun,
The syllables be said and said again:
Time shall belong to man.

76

ALL THAT I OWE THE FELLOWS OF THE GRAVE

All that I owe the fellows of the grave
And all the dead bequeath from pale estates
Lies in the fortuned bone, the flask of blood,
Like senna stirs along the ravaged roots.
O all I owe is all the flesh inherits,
My fathers' loves that pull upon my nerves,
My sisters' tears that sing upon my head,
My brothers' blood that salts my open wounds.

Heir to the scalding veins that hold love's drop,
My fallen filled, that had the hint of death,
Heir to the telling senses that alone
Acquaint the flesh with a remembered itch,
I round this heritage as rounds the sun
His winy sky, and, as the candle's moon,
Cast light upon my weather. I am heir

To women who have twisted their last smile,
To children who were suckled on a plague,
To young adorers dying on a kiss.
All such disease I doctor in my blood,
And all such love's a shrub sown in the breath.

Then look, my eyes, upon this bonebound fortune
And browse upon the postures of the dead;
All night and day I eye the ragged globe
Through periscopes rightsighted from the grave;
All night and day I wander in these same
Wax clothes that wax upon the ageing ribs;
All night my fortune slumbers in its sheet.
Then look, my heart, upon the scarlet trove,
And look, my grain, upon the falling wheat;
All night my fortune slumbers in its sheet.

77

HERE LIE THE BEASTS

Here lie the beasts of man and here I feast,
The dead man said,
And silently I milk the devil's breast.
Here spring the silent venoms of his blood,
Here clings the meat to sever from his side.
Hell's in the dust.

Here lies the beast of man and here his angels,
The dead man said,
And silently I milk the buried flowers.
Here drips a silent honey in my shroud,
Here slips the ghost who made of my pale bed
The heaven's house.

LIGHT BREAKS WHERE NO SUN SHINES

Light breaks where no sun shines;
Where no sea runs, the waters of the heart
Push in their tides;
And, broken ghosts with glow-worms in their heads,
The things of light
File through the flesh where no flesh decks the bones.

A candle in the thighs
Warms youth and seed and burns the seeds of age;
Where no seed stirs,
The fruit of man unwrinkles in the stars,
Bright as a fig;
Where no wax is, the candle shows its hairs.

Dawn breaks behind the eyes;
From poles of skull and toe the windy blood
Slides like a sea;
Nor fenced, nor staked, the gushers of the sky
Spout to the rod
Divining in a smile the oil of tears.

Night in the sockets rounds,
Like some pitch moon, the limit of the globes;
Day lights the bone;
Where no cold is, the skinning gales unpin
The winter's robes;
The film of spring is hanging from the lids.

Light breaks on secret lots,
On tips of thought where thoughts smell in the rain;
When logics die,
The secret of the soil grows through the eye,
And blood jumps in the sun;
Above the waste allotments the dawn halts.

A LETTER TO MY AUNT
DISCUSSING THE CORRECT APPROACH TO MODERN POETRY

To you, my aunt, who would explore
The literary Chankley Bore,
The paths are hard, for you are not
A literary Hottentot
But just a kind and cultured dame
Who knows not Eliot (to her shame).
Fie on you, aunt, that you should see
No genius in David G.,
No elemental form and sound
In T.S.E. and Ezra Pound.
Fie on you, aunt! I'll show you how
To elevate your middle brow,
And how to scale and see the sights
From modernist Parnassian heights.

First buy a hat, no Paris model
But one the Swiss wear when they yodel,
A bowler thing with one or two
Feathers to conceal the view;
And then in sandals walk the street
(All modern painters use their feet
For painting, on their canvas strips,
Their wives or mothers minus hips).

Perhaps it would be best if you
Created something very new,
A dirty novel done in Erse
Or written backwards in Welsh verse,
Or paintings on the backs of vests,
Or Sanskrit psalms on lepers' chests.

But if this proved imposs-i-ble
Perhaps it would be just as well,
For you could then write what you please,
And modern verse is done with ease.

Do not forget that 'limpet' rhymes
With 'strumpet' in these troubled times,
And commas are the worst of crimes;
Few understand the works of Cummings,
And few James Joyce's mental slummings,
And few young Auden's coded chatter;
But then it is the few that matter.
Never be lucid, never state,
If you would be regarded great,
The simplest thought or sentiment,
(For thought, we know, is decadent);
Never omit such vital words
As belly, genitals, and ——,
For these are things that play a part
(And what a part) in all good art.
Remember this: each rose is wormy,
And every lovely woman's germy;
Remember this: that love depends
On how the Gallic letter bends;
Remember, too, that life is hell
And even heaven has a smell
Of putrefying angels who
Make deadly whoopee in the blue.
These things remembered, what can stop
A poet going to the top?

A final word: before you start
The convulsions of your art,
Remove your brains, take out your heart;

Minus these curses, you can be
A genius like David G.

Take courage, aunt, and send your stuff
To Geoffrey Grigson with my luff,
And may I yet live to admire
How well your poems light the fire.

80

SEE, SAYS THE LIME

See, says the lime, my wicked milks
I put round ribs that packed their heart,
And elbowed veins that, nudging blood,
Roused it to fire;
Once in this clay fenced by the sticks
That starry fence the clay of light
The howling spirit shaped a god
Of death's undoer.

On these blue lips, the lime remarks,
The wind of kisses sealed a pact
That leaping veins threw to the wind
And brains turned sour;
The blood got up as red as wax
As kisses froze the waxing thought,
The spirit racked its muscles and
The loins cried murder.

The strings of fire choked his sex
And tied an iris in his throat
To burst into a hanging land
Where flesh's fever
Itched on the hangman's silks;

[85]

The brains of death undid the knot
Before the blood and flame were twined
In love's last collar.
See, says the lime, around these wrecks
Of growing bones the muscles slid;
I chalked upon the breastbone's slate
And ran a river
Up through the fingers' cracks;
The milk of death, I filled the hand
That drove my stuff through skin and gut;
Death's death's undoer.

THIS BREAD I BREAK

This bread I break was once the oat,
This wine upon a foreign tree
Plunged in its fruit;
Man in the day or wind at night
Laid the crops low, broke the grape's joy.

Once in this wine the summer blood
Knocked in the flesh that decked the vine,
Once in this bread
The oat was merry in the wind;
Man broke the sun, pulled the wind down.

This flesh you break, this blood you let
Make desolation in the vein,
Were oat and grape
Born of the sensual root and sap;
My wine you drink, my bread you snap.

YOUR PAIN SHALL BE A MUSIC

Your pain shall be a music in your string
And fill the mouths of heaven with your tongue
Your pain shall be
O my unborn
A vein of mine
Made fast by me.

Your string shall stretch a gully twixt the thumbs
Whose flaming blood shall rub it at the rims
Your pain shall be
O my unsown
A ragged vein
Twixt you and me.

Your pain shall be a meaning in your lips
As milk shall be a music in the paps
Your pain shall be
O my unknown
A stream of mine
Not milked by me.

Your pain shall not unmilk you of the food
That drops to make a music in your blood
Your pain shall be
O my undone
Flesh blood and bone
Surrounding me.

A PROCESS IN THE WEATHER OF THE HEART

A process in the weather of the heart
Turns damp to dry; the golden shot
Storms in the freezing tomb.
A weather in the quarter of the veins
Turns night to day; blood in their suns
Lights up the living worm.

A process in the eye forewarns
The bones of blindness; and the womb
Drives in a death as life leaks out.

A darkness in the weather of the eye
Is half its light; the fathomed sea
Breaks on unangled land.
The seed that makes a forest of the loin
Forks half its fruit; and half drops down,
Slow in a sleeping wind.

A weather in the flesh and bone
Is damp and dry; the quick and dead
Move like two ghosts before the eye.

A process in the weather of the world
Turns ghost to ghost; each mothered child
Sits in their double shade.
A process blows the moon into the sun,
Pulls down the shabby curtains of the skin;
And the heart gives up its dead.

OUR EUNUCH DREAMS

I

Our eunuch dreams, all seedless in the light,
Of light and love, the tempers of the heart,
Whack their boys' limbs,
And, winding-footed in their shawl and sheet,
Groom the dark brides, the widows of the night
Fold in their arms.

The shades of girls, all flavoured from their shrouds,
When sunlight goes are sundered from the worm,
The bones of men, the broken in their beds,
By midnight pulleys that unhouse the tomb.

II

In this our age the gunman and his moll,
Two one-dimensioned ghosts, love on a reel,
Strange to our solid eye,
And speak their midnight nothings as they swell;
When cameras shut they hurry to their hole
Down in the yard of day.

They dance between their arclamps and our skull,
Impose their shots, throwing the nights away;
We watch the show of shadows kiss or kill,
Flavoured of celluloid give love the lie.

III

Which is the world? Of our two sleepings, which
Shall fall awake when cures and their itch
Raise up this red-eyed earth?

[89]

Pack off the shapes of daylight and their starch,
The sunny gentlemen, the Welshing rich,
Or drive the night-geared forth.

The photograph is married to the eye,
Grafts on its bride one-sided skins of truth;
The dream has sucked the sleeper of his faith
That shrouded men might marrow as they fly.

IV

This is the world: the lying likeness of
Our strips of stuff that tatter as we move
Loving and being loth;
The dream that kicks the buried from their sack
And lets their trash be honoured as the quick.
This is the world. Have faith.

For we shall be a shouter like the cock,
Blowing the old dead back; our shots shall smack
The image from the plates;
And we shall be fit fellows for a life,
And who remain shall flower as they love,
Praise to our faring hearts.

85

WHERE ONCE THE WATERS OF YOUR FACE

Where once the waters of your face
Spun to my screws, your dry ghost blows,
The dead turns up its eye;
Where once the mermen through your ice
Pushed up their hair, the dry wind steers
Through salt and root and roe.

[90]

Where once your green knots sank their splice
Into the tided cord, there goes
The green unraveller,
His scissors oiled, his knife hung loose
To cut the channels at their source
And lay the wet fruits low.

Invisible, your clocking tides
Break on the lovebeds of the weeds;
The weed of love's left dry;
There round about your stones the shades
Of children go who, from their voids,
Cry to the dolphined sea.

Dry as a tomb, your coloured lids
Shall not be latched while magic glides
Sage on the earth and sky;
There shall be corals in your beds,
There shall be serpents in your tides,
Till all our sea-faiths die.

86

I SEE THE BOYS OF SUMMER

I

I see the boys of summer in their ruin
Lay the gold tithings barren,
Setting no store by harvest, freeze the soils;
There in their heat the winter floods
Of frozen loves they fetch their girls,
And drown the cargoed apples in their tides.

These boys of light are curdlers in their folly,
Sour the boiling honey;
The jacks of frost they finger in the hives;
There in the sun the frigid threads
Of doubt and dark they feed their nerves;
The signal moon is zero in their voids.

I see the summer children in their mothers
Split up the brawned womb's weathers,
Divide the night and day with fairy thumbs;
There in the deep with quartered shades
Of sun and moon they paint their dams
As sunlight paints the shelling of their heads.

I see that from these boys shall men of nothing
Stature by seedy shifting,
Or lame the air with leaping from its heats;
There from their hearts the dogdayed pulse
Of love and light bursts in their throats.
O see the pulse of summer in the ice.

II

But seasons must be challenged or they totter
Into a chiming quarter
Where, punctual as death, we ring the stars;
There, in his night, the black-tongued bells
The sleepy man of winter pulls,
Nor blows back moon-and-midnight as she blows.

We are the dark deniers, let us summon
Death from a summer woman,
A muscling life from lovers in their cramp,
From the fair dead who flush the sea
The bright-eyed worm on Davy's lamp,
And from the planted womb the man of straw.

We summer boys in this four-winded spinning,
Green of the seaweeds' iron,
Hold up the noisy sea and drop her birds,
Pick the world's ball of wave and froth
To choke the deserts with her tides,
And comb the county gardens for a wreath.

In spring we cross our foreheads with the holly,
Heigh ho the blood and berry,
And nail the merry squires to the trees;
Here love's damp muscle dries and dies,
Here break a kiss in no love's quarry.
O see the poles of promise in the boys.

III

I see you boys of summer in your ruin.
Man in his maggot's barren.
And boys are full and foreign in the pouch.
I am the man your father was.
We are the sons of flint and pitch.
O see the poles are kissing as they cross.

87

IN THE BEGINNING

In the beginning was the three-pointed star,
One smile of light across the empty face;
One bough of bone across the rooting air,
The substance forked that marrowed the first sun;
And, burning ciphers on the round of space,
Heaven and hell mixed as they spun.

In the beginning was the pale signature,
Three-syllabled and starry as the smile;
And after came the imprints on the water,
Stamp of the minted face upon the moon;
The blood that touched the crosstree and the grail
Touched the first cloud and left a sign.

In the beginning was the mounting fire
That set alight the weathers from a spark,
A three-eyed, red-eyed spark, blunt as a flower;
Life rose and spouted from the rolling seas,
Burst in the roots, pumped from the earth and rock
The secret oils that drive the grass.

In the beginning was the word, the word
That from the solid bases of the light
Abstracted all the letters of the void;
And from the cloudy bases of the breath
The word flowed up, translating to the heart
First characters of birth and death.

In the beginning was the secret brain.
The brain was celled and soldered in the thought
Before the pitch was forking to a sun;
Before the veins were shaking in their sieve,
Blood shot and scattered to the winds of light
The ribbed original of love.

88

IF I WERE TICKLED BY THE RUB OF LOVE

If I were tickled by the rub of love,
A rooking girl who stole me for her side,
Broke through her straws, breaking my bandaged string,

If the red tickle as the cattle calve
Still set to scratch a laughter from my lung,
I would not fear the apple nor the flood
Nor the bad blood of spring.

Shall it be male or female? say the cells,
And drop the plum like fire from the flesh.
If I were tickled by the hatching hair,
The winging bone that sprouted in the heels,
The itch of man upon the baby's thigh,
I would not fear the gallows nor the axe
Nor the crossed sticks of war.

Shall it be male or female? say the fingers
That chalk the walls with green girls and their men.
I would not fear the muscling-in of love
If I were tickled by the urchin hungers
Rehearsing heat upon a raw-edged nerve.
I would not fear the devil in the loin
Nor the outspoken grave.

If I were tickled by the lovers' rub
That wipes away not crow's-foot nor the lock
Of sick old manhood on the fallen jaws,
Time and the crabs and the sweethearting crib
Would leave me cold as butter for the flies,
The sea of scums could drown me as it broke
Dead on the sweethearts' toes.

This world is half the devil's and my own,
Daft with the drug that's smoking in a girl
And curling round the bud that forks her eye.
An old man's shank one-marrowed with my bone,
And all the herrings smelling in the sea,
I sit and watch the worm beneath my nail
Wearing the quick away.

And that's the rub, the only rub that tickles.
The knobbly ape that swings along his sex
From damp love-darkness and the nurse's twist
Can never raise the midnight of a chuckle,
Nor when he finds a beauty in the breast
Of lover, mother, lovers, or his six
Feet in the rubbing dust.

And what's the rub? Death's feather on the nerve?
Your mouth, my love, the thistle in the kiss?
My Jack of Christ born thorny on the tree?
The words of death are dryer than his stiff,
My wordy wounds are printed with your hair.
I would be tickled by the rub that is:
Man be my metaphor.

89

TWELVE

That the sum sanity might add to naught
And words fall crippled from the slaving lips,
Girls take to broomsticks when the thief of night
Has stolen the starved babies from their laps,
I would enforce the black apparelled cries,
Speak like a hungry parson of the manna,
Add one more nail of praise on to the cross,
And talk of light to a mad miner.
I would be woven a religious shape;
As fleeced as they bow lowly with the sheep,
My house would fall like bread about my homage;
And I would choke the heavens with my hymn
That men might see the devil in the crumb
And the death in a starving image.

WHEN ONCE THE TWILIGHT LOCKS NO LONGER

When once the twilight locks no longer
Locked in the long worm of my finger
Nor damned the sea that sped about my fist,
The mouth of time sucked, like a sponge,
The milky acid on each hinge,
And swallowed dry the waters of the breast.

When the galactic sea was sucked
And all the dry seabed unlocked,
I sent my creature scouting on the globe,
That globe itself of hair and bone
That, sewn to me by nerve and brain,
Had stringed my flask of matter to his rib.

My fuses timed to charge his heart,
He blew like powder to the light
And held a little sabbath with the sun,
But when the stars, assuming shape,
Drew in his eyes the straws of sleep,
He drowned his father's magics in a dream.

All issue armoured, of the grave,
The redhaired cancer still alive,
The cataracted eyes that filmed their cloth;
Some dead undid their bushy jaws,
And bags of blood let out their flies;
He had by heart the Christ-cross-row of death.

Sleep navigates the tides of time;
The dry Sargasso of the tomb
Gives up its dead to such a working sea;

And sleep rolls mute above the beds
Where fishes' food is fed the shades
Who periscope through flowers to the sky.

When once the twilight screws were turned,
And mother milk was stiff as sand,
I sent my own ambassador to light;
By trick or chance he fell asleep
And conjured up a carcass shape
To rob me of my fluids in his heart.

Awake, my sleeper, to the sun,
A worker in the morning town,
And leave the poppied pickthank where he lies;
The fences of the light are down,
All but the briskest riders thrown,
And worlds hang on the trees.

91

ESPECIALLY WHEN THE OCTOBER WIND

Especially when the October wind
With frosty fingers punishes my hair,
Caught by the crabbing sun I walk on fire
And cast a shadow crab upon the land,
By the sea's side, hearing the noise of birds,
Hearing the raven cough in winter sticks,
My busy heart who shudders as she talks
Sheds the syllabic blood and drains her words.

Shut, too, in a tower of words, I mark
On the horizon walking like the trees
The wordy shapes of women, and the rows
Of the star-gestured children in the park.

Some let me make you of the vowelled beeches,
Some of the oaken voices, from the roots
Of many a thorny shire tell you notes,
Some let me make you of the water's speeches.

Behind a pot of ferns the wagging clock
Tells me the hour's word, the neural meaning
Flies on the shafted disk, declaims the morning
And tells the windy weather in the cock.
Some let me make you of the meadow's signs;
The signal grass that tells me all I know
Breaks with the wormy winter through the eye.
Some let me tell you of the raven's sins.

Especially when the October wind
(Some let me make you of autumnal spells,
The spider-tongued, and the loud hill of Wales)
With fists of turnips punishes the land,
Some let me make you of the heartless words.
The heart is drained that, spelling in the scurry
Of chemic blood, warned of the coming fury.
By the sea's side hear the dark-vowelled birds.

92

WHEN, LIKE A RUNNING GRAVE

When, like a running grave, time tracks you down,
Your calm and cuddled is a scythe of hairs,
Love in her gear is slowly through the house,
Up naked stairs, a turtle in a hearse,
Hauled to the dome,

Comes, like a scissors stalking, tailor age,
Deliver me who, timid in my tribe,
Of love am barer than Cadaver's trap
Robbed of the foxy tongue, his footed tape
Of the bone inch,

Deliver me, my masters, head and heart,
Heart of Cadaver's candle waxes thin,
When blood, spade-handed, and the logic time
Drive children up like bruises to the thumb,
From maid and head,

For, sunday faced, with dusters in my glove,
Chaste and the chaser, man with the cockshut eye,
I, that time's jacket or the coat of ice
May fail to fasten with a virgin o
In the straight grave,

Stride through Cadaver's country in my force,
My pickbrain masters morsing on the stone
Despair of blood, faith in the maiden's slime,
Halt among eunuchs, and the nitric stain
On fork and face.

Time is a foolish fancy, time and fool.
No, no, you lover skull, descending hammer
Descends, my masters, on the entered honour.
You hero skull, Cadaver in the hangar
Tells the stick, 'fail'.

Joy is no knocking nation, sir and madam,
The cancer's fusion, or the summer feather
Lit on the cuddled tree, the cross of fever,
Nor city tar and subway bored to foster
Man through macadam.

I damp the waxlights in your tower dome.
Joy is the knock of dust, Cadaver's shoot
Of bud of Adam through his boxy shift,
Love's twilit nation and the skull of state,
Sir, is your doom.

Everything ends, the tower ending and,
(Have with the house of wind), the leaning scene,
Ball of the foot depending from the sun,
(Give, summer, over), the cemented skin,
The actions' end.

All, men my madmen, the unwholesome wind
With whistler's cough contages, time on track
Shapes in a cinder death; love for his trick,
Happy Cadaver's hunger as you take
The kissproof world.

93

I FELLOWED SLEEP

I fellowed sleep who kissed me in the brain,
Let fall the tear of time; the sleeper's eye,
Shifting to light, turned on me like a moon.
So, planing-heeled, I flew along my man
And dropped on dreaming and the upward sky.

I fled the earth and, naked, climbed the weather,
Reaching a second ground far from the stars;
And there we wept, I and a ghostly other,
My mothers-eyed, upon the tops of trees;
I fled that ground as lightly as a feather.

'My fathers' globe knocks on its nave and sings.'
'This that we tread was, too, your fathers' land.'

'But this we tread bears the angelic gangs,
Sweet are their fathered faces in their wings.'
'These are but dreaming men. Breathe, and they fade.'

Faded my elbow ghost, the mothers-eyed,
As, blowing on the angels, I was lost
On that cloud coast to each grave-gabbing shade;
I blew the dreaming fellows to their bed
Where still they sleep unknowing of their ghost.

Then all the matter of the living air
Raised up a voice, and, climbing on the words,
I spelt my vision with a hand and hair,
How light the sleeping on this soily star,
How deep the waking in the worlded clouds.

There grows the hours' ladder to the sun,
Each rung a love or losing to the last,
The inches monkeyed by the blood of man.
An old, mad man still climbing in his ghost,
My fathers' ghost is climbing in the rain.

94

I DREAMED MY GENESIS

I dreamed my genesis in sweat of sleep, breaking
Through the rotating shell, strong
As motor muscle on the drill, driving
Through vision and the girdered nerve,

From limbs that had the measure of the worm, shuffled
Off from the creasing flesh, filed
Through all the irons in the grass, metal
Of suns in the man-melting night.

Heir to the scalding veins that hold love's drop, costly
A creature in my bones I
Rounded my globe of heritage, journey
In bottom gear through night-geared man.

I dreamed my genesis and died again, shrapnel
Rammed in the marching heart, hole
In the stitched wound and clotted wind, muzzled
Death on the mouth that ate the gas.

Sharp in my second death I marked the hills, harvest
Of hemlock and the blades, rust
My blood upon the tempered dead, forcing
My second struggling from the grass.

And power was contagious in my birth, second
Rise of the skeleton and
Rerobing of the naked ghost. Manhood
Spat up from the resuffered pain.

I dreamed my genesis in sweat of death, fallen
Twice in the feeding sea, grown
Stale of Adam's brine until, vision
Of new man strength, I seek the sun.

95

MY WORLD IS PYRAMID

I

Half of the fellow father as he doubles
His sea-sucked Adam in the hollow hulk,
Half of the fellow mother as she dabbles
To-morrow's diver in her horny milk,
Bisected shadows on the thunder's bone
Bolt for the salt unborn.

The fellow half was frozen as it bubbled
Corrosive spring out of the iceberg's crop,
The fellow seed and shadow as it babbled
The swing of milk was tufted in the pap,
For half of love was planted in the lost,
And the unplanted ghost.

The broken halves are fellowed in a cripple,
The crutch that marrow taps upon their sleep,
Limp in the street of sea, among the rabble
Of tide-tongued heads and bladders in the deep,
And stake the sleepers in the savage grave
That the vampire laugh.

The patchwork halves were cloven as they scudded
The wild pigs' wood, and slime upon the trees,
Sucking the dark, kissed on the cyanide,
And loosed the braiding adders from their hairs;
Rotating halves are horning as they drill
The arterial angel.

What colour is glory? death's feather? tremble
The halves that pierce the pin's point in the air,
And prick the thumb-stained heaven through the thimble.
The ghost is dumb that stammered in the straw,
The ghost that hatched his havoc as he flew
Blinds their cloud-tracking eye.

II

My world is pyramid. The padded mummer
Weeps on the desert ochre and the salt
Incising summer.
My Egypt's armour buckling in its sheet,
I scrape through resin to a starry bone
And a blood parhelion.

My world is cypress, and an English valley.
I piece my flesh that rattled on the yards
Red in an Austrian volley.
I hear, through dead men's drums, the riddled lads,
Strewing their bowels from a hill of bones,
Cry Eloi to the guns.

My grave is watered by the crossing Jordan.
The Arctic scut, and basin of the South,
Drip on my dead house garden.
Who seek me landward, marking in my mouth
The straws of Asia, lose me as I turn
Through the Atlantic corn.

The fellow halves that, cloven as they swivel
On casting tides, are tangled in the shells,
Bearding the unborn devil,
Bleed from my burning fork and smell my heels.
The tongues of heaven gossip as I glide
Binding my angel's hood.

Who blows death's feather? What glory is colour?
I blow the stammel feather in the vein.
The loin is glory in a working pallor.
My clay unsuckled and my salt unborn,
The secret child, I shift about the sea
Dry in the half-tracked thigh.

ALL ALL AND ALL THE DRY WORLDS LEVER

I

All all and all the dry worlds lever,
Stage of the ice, the solid ocean,
All from the oil, the pound of lava.
City of spring, the governed flower,
Turns in the earth that turns the ashen
Towns around on a wheel of fire.

How now my flesh, my naked fellow,
Dug of the sea, the glanded morrow,
Worm in the scalp, the staked and fallow.
All all and all, the corpse's lover,
Skinny as sin, the foaming marrow,
All of the flesh, the dry worlds lever.

II

Fear not the working world, my mortal,
Fear not the flat, synthetic blood,
Nor the heart in the ribbing metal.
Fear not the tread, the seeded milling,
The trigger and scythe, the bridal blade,
Nor the flint in the lover's mauling.

Man of my flesh, the jawbone riven,
Know now the flesh's lock and vice,
And the cage for the scythe-eyed raven.
Know, O my bone, the jointed lever,
Fear not the screws that turn the voice,
And the face to the driven lover.

III

All all and all the dry worlds couple,
Ghost with her ghost, contagious man
With the womb of his shapeless people.
All that shapes from the caul and suckle,
Stroke of mechanical flesh on mine,
Square in these worlds the mortal circle.

Flower, flower the people's fusion,
O light in zenith, the coupled bud,
And the flame in the flesh's vision.
Out of the sea, the drive of oil,
Socket and grave, the brassy blood,
Flower, flower, all all and all.

97

GRIEF THIEF OF TIME

Grief thief of time crawls off,
The moon-drawn grave, with the seafaring years,
The knave of pain steals off
The sea-halved faith that blew time to his knees,
The old forget the cries,
Lean time on tide and times the wind stood rough,
Call back the castaways
Riding the sea light on a sunken path,
The old forget the grief,
Hack of the cough, the hanging albatross,
Cast back the bone of youth
And salt-eyed stumble bedward where she lies

[107]

Who tossed the high tide in a time of stories
And timelessly lies loving with the thief.

Now Jack my fathers let the time-faced crook,
Death flashing from his sleeve,
With swag of bubbles in a seedy sack
Sneak down the stallion grave,
Bull's-eye the outlaw through a eunuch crack
And free the twin-boxed grief,
No silver whistles chase him down the weeks'
Dayed peaks to day to death,
These stolen bubbles have the bites of snakes
And the undead eye-teeth,
No third eye probe into a rainbow's sex
That bridged the human halves,
All shall remain and on the graveward gulf
Shape with my fathers' thieves.

98

I, IN MY INTRICATE IMAGE

I

I, in my intricate image, stride on two levels,
Forged in man's minerals, the brassy orator
Laying my ghost in metal,
The scales of this twin world tread on the double,
My half ghost in armour hold hard in death's corridor,
To my man-iron sidle.

Beginning with doom in the bulb, the spring unravels,
Bright as her spinning-wheels, the colic season
Worked on a world of petals;
She threads off the sap and needles, blood and bubble

Casts to the pine roots, raising man like a mountain
Out of the naked entrail.

Beginning with doom in the ghost, and the springing marvels,
Images of images, my metal phantom
Forcing forth through the harebell,
My man of leaves and the bronze root, mortal, unmortal,
I, in my fusion of rose and male motion,
Create this twin miracle.

This is the fortune of manhood: the natural peril,
A steeplejack tower, bonerailed and masterless,
No death more natural;
Thus the shadowless man or ox, and the pictured devil,
In seizure of silence commit the dead nuisance:
The natural parallel.

My images stalk the trees and the slant sap's tunnel,
No tread more perilous, the green steps and spire
Mount on man's footfall,
I with the wooden insect in the tree of nettles,
In the glass bed of grapes with snail and flower,
Hearing the weather fall.

Intricate manhood of ending, the invalid rivals,
Voyaging clockwise off the symboled harbour,
Finding the water final,
On the consumptives' terrace taking their two farewells,
Sail on the level, the departing adventure,
To the sea-blown arrival.

II

They climb the country pinnacle,
Twelve winds encounter by the white host at pasture,
Corner the mounted meadows in the hill corral;
They see the squirrel stumble,
The haring snail go giddily round the flower,
A quarrel of weathers and trees in the windy spiral.

As they dive, the dust settles,
The cadaverous gravels, falls thick and steadily,
The highroad of water where the seabear and mackerel
Turn the long sea arterial
Turning a petrol face blind to the enemy
Turning the riderless dead by the channel wall.

(Death instrumental,
Splitting the long eye open, and the spiral turnkey,
Your corkscrew grave centred in navel and nipple,
The neck of the nostril,
Under the mask and the ether, they, making bloody
The tray of knives, the antiseptic funeral,

Bring out the black patrol,
Your monstrous officers and the decaying army,
The sexton sentinel, garrisoned under thistles,
A cock-on-a-dunghill
Crowing to Lazarus the morning is vanity,
Dust be your saviour under the conjured soil.)

As they drown, the chime travels,
Sweetly the diver's bell in the steeple of spindrift
Rings out the Dead Sea scale;
And, clapped in water till the triton dangles,
Strung by the flaxen whale-weed, from the hangman's raft,
Hear they the salt glass breakers and the tongues of burial.

(Turn the sea-spindle lateral,
The grooved land rotating, that the stylus of lightning
Dazzle this face of voices on the moon-turned table,
Let the wax disk babble
Shames and the damp dishonours, the relic scraping.
These are your years' recorders. The circular world stands
   still.)

III

They suffer the undead water where the turtle nibbles,
Come unto sea-stuck towers, at the fibre scaling,
The flight of the carnal skull
And the cell-stepped thimble;
Suffer, my topsy-turvies, that a double angel
Sprout from the stony lockers like a tree on Aran.

Be by your one ghost pierced, his pointed ferrule,
Brass and the bodiless image, on a stick of folly
Star-set at Jacob's angle,
Smoke hill and hophead's valley.
And the five-fathomed Hamlet on his father's coral,
Thrusting the tom-thumb vision up the iron mile.

Suffer the slash of vision by the fin-green stubble,
Be by the ships' sea broken at the manstring anchored
The stoved bones' voyage downward
In the shipwreck of muscle;
Give over, lovers, locking, and the seawax struggle,
Love like a mist or fire through the bed of eels.

And in the pincers of the boiling circle,
The sea and instrument, nicked in the locks of time,
My great blood's iron single
In the pouring town,
I, in a wind on fire, from green Adam's cradle,
No man more magical, clawed out the crocodile.

Man was the scales, the death birds on enamel,
Tail, Nile, and snout, a saddler of the rushes,
Time in the hourless houses
Shaking the sea-hatched skull,
And, as for oils and ointments on the flying grail,
All-hollowed man wept for his white apparel.

Man was Cadaver's masker, the harnessing mantle,
Windily master of man was the rotten fathom,
My ghost in his metal neptune
Forged in man's mineral.
This was the god of beginning in the intricate seawhirl,
And my images roared and rose on heaven's hill.

99

DO YOU NOT FATHER ME

Do you not father me, nor the erected arm
For my tall tower's sake cast in her stone?
Do you not mother me, nor, as I am,
The lovers' house, lie suffering my stain?
Do you not sister me, nor the erected crime
For my tall turrets carry as your sin?
Do you not brother me, nor, as you climb,
Adore my windows for their summer scene?

Am I not father, too, and the ascending boy,
The boy of woman and the wanton starer
Marking the flesh and summer in the bay?
Am I not sister, too, who is my saviour?
Am I not all of you by the directed sea
Where bird and shell are babbling in my tower?
Am I not you who front the tidy shore,
Nor roof of sand, nor yet the towering tiler?

You are all these, said she who gave me the long suck,
All these, he said who sacked the children's town,
Up rose the Abraham-man, mad for my sake,
They said, who hacked and humoured, they were mine.

I am, the tower told, felled by a timeless stroke,
Who razed my wooden folly stands aghast,
For man-begetters in the dry-as-paste,
The ringed-sea ghost, rise grimly from the wrack.

Do you not father me on the destroying sand?
You are your sisters' sire, said seaweedy,
The salt sucked dam and darlings of the land
Who play the proper gentleman and lady.
Shall I still be love's house on the widdershin earth,
Woe to the windy masons at my shelter?
Love's house, they answer, and the tower death
Lie all unknowing of the grave sin-eater.

100

HOW SOON THE SERVANT SUN

How soon the servant sun,
(Sir morrow mark),
Can time unriddle, and the cupboard stone,
(Fog has a bone
He'll trumpet into meat),
Unshelve that all my gristles have a gown
And the naked egg stand straight,

Sir morrow at his sponge,
(The wound records),
The nurse of giants by the cut sea basin,
(Fog by his spring
Soaks up the sewing tides),
Tells you and you, my masters, as his strange
Man morrow blows through food.

[113]

All nerves to serve the sun,
The rite of light,
A claw I question from the mouse's bone,
The long-tailed stone
Trap I with coil and sheet,
Let the soil squeal I am the biting man
And the velvet dead inch out.

How soon my level, lord,
(Sir morrow stamps
Two heels of water on the floor of seed),
Shall raise a lamp
Or spirit up a cloud,
Erect a walking centre in the shroud,
Invisible on the stump

A leg as long as trees,
This inward sir,
Mister and master, darkness for his eyes,
The womb-eyed, cries,
And all sweet hell, deaf as an hour's ear,
Blasts back the trumpet voice.

101

A GRIEF AGO

A grief ago,
She who was who I hold, the fats and flower,
Or, water-lammed, from the scythe-sided thorn,
Hell wind and sea,
A stem cementing, wrestled up the tower,
Rose maid and male,
Or, masted venus, through the paddler's bowl
Sailed up the sun;

Who is my grief,
A chrysalis unwrinkling on the iron,
Wrenched by my fingerman, the leaden bud
Shot through the leaf,
Was who was folded on the rod the aaron
Rose cast to plague,
The horn and ball of water on the frog
Housed in the side.

And she who lies,
Like exodus a chapter from the garden,
Brand of the lily's anger on her ring,
Tugged through the days
Her ropes of heritage, the wars of pardon,
On field and sand
The twelve triangles of the cherub wind
Engraving going.

Who then is she,
She holding me? The people's sea drives on her,
Drives out the father from the caesared camp;
The dens of shape
Shape all her whelps with the long voice of water,
That she I have,
The country-handed grave boxed into love,
Rise before dark.

The night is near,
A nitric shape that leaps her, time and acid;
I tell her this: before the suncock cast
Her bone to fire,
Let her inhale her dead, through seed and solid
Draw in their seas,
So cross her hand with their grave gipsy eyes,
And close her fist.

SHOULD LANTERNS SHINE

Should lanterns shine, the holy face,
Caught in an octagon of unaccustomed light,
Would wither up, and any boy of love
Look twice before he fell from grace.
The features in their private dark
Are formed of flesh, but let the false day come
And from her lips the faded pigments fall,
The mummy cloths expose an ancient breast.

I have been told to reason by the heart,
But heart, like head, leads helplessly;
I have been told to reason by the pulse,
And, when it quickens, alter the actions' pace
Till field and roof lie level and the same
So fast I move defying time, the quiet gentleman
Whose beard wags in Egyptian wind.

I have heard many years of telling,
And many years should see some change.

The ball I threw while playing in the park
Has not yet reached the ground.

ALTARWISE BY OWL-LIGHT

I

Altarwise by owl-light in the half-way house
The gentleman lay graveward with his furies;
Abaddon in the hangnail cracked from Adam,

And, from his fork, a dog among the fairies,
The atlas-eater with a jaw for news,
Bit out the mandrake with to-morrow's scream.
Then, penny-eyed, that gentleman of wounds,
Old cock from nowheres and the heaven's egg,
With bones unbuttoned to the half-way winds,
Hatched from the windy salvage on one leg,
Scraped at my cradle in a walking word
That night of time under the Christward shelter:
I am the long world's gentleman, he said,
And share my bed with Capricorn and Cancer.

II

Death is all metaphors, shape in one history;
The child that sucketh long is shooting up,
The planet-ducted pelican of circles
Weans on an artery the gender's strip;
Child of the short spark in a shapeless country
Soon sets alight a long stick from the cradle;
The horizontal cross-bones of Abaddon,
You by the cavern over the black stairs,
Rung bone and blade, the verticals of Adam,
And, manned by midnight, Jacob to the stars.
Hairs of your head, then said the hollow agent,
Are but the roots of nettles and of feathers
Over these groundworks thrusting through a pavement
And hemlock-headed in the wood of weathers.

III

First there was the lamb on knocking knees
And three dead seasons on a climbing grave
That Adam's wether in the flock of horns,
Butt of the tree-tailed worm that mounted Eve,
Horned down with skullfoot and the skull of toes
On thunderous pavements in the garden time;

Rip of the vaults, I took my marrow-ladle
Out of the wrinkled undertaker's van,
And, Rip Van Winkle from a timeless cradle,
Dipped me breast-deep in the descending bone;
The black ram, shuffling of the year, old winter,
Alone alive among his mutton fold,
We rung our weathering changes on the ladder,
Said the antipodes, and twice spring chimed.

IV

What is the metre of the dictionary?
The size of genesis? the short spark's gender?
Shade without shape? the shape of Pharaoh's echo?
(My shape of age nagging the wounded whisper.)
Which sixth of wind blew out the burning gentry?
(Questions are hunchbacks to the poker marrow.)
What of a bamboo man among your acres?
Corset the boneyards for a crooked boy?
Button your bodice on a hump of splinters,
My camel's eyes will needle through the shroud.
Love's reflection of the mushroom features,
Stills snapped by night in the bread-sided field,
Once close-up smiling in the wall of pictures,
Arc-lamped thrown back upon the cutting flood.

V

And from the windy West came two-gunned Gabriel,
From Jesu's sleeve trumped up the king of spots,
The sheath-decked jacks, queen with a shuffled heart;
Said the fake gentleman in suit of spades,
Black-tongued and tipsy from salvation's bottle.
Rose my Byzantine Adam in the night.
For loss of blood I fell on Ishmael's plain,
Under the milky mushrooms slew my hunger,
A climbing sea from Asia had me down

And Jonah's Moby snatched me by the hair,
Cross-stroked salt Adam to the frozen angel
Pin-legged on pole-hills with a black medusa
By waste seas where the white bear quoted Virgil
And sirens singing from our lady's sea-straw.

VI

Cartoon of slashes on the tide-traced crater,
He in a book of water tallow-eyed
By lava's light split through the oyster vowels
And burned sea silence on a wick of words.
Pluck, cock, my sea eye, said medusa's scripture,
Lop, love, my fork tongue, said the pin-hilled nettle;
And love plucked out the stinging siren's eye,
Old cock from nowheres lopped the minstrel tongue
Till tallow I blew from the wax's tower
The fats of midnight when the salt was singing;
Adam, time's joker, on a witch of cardboard
Spelt out the seven seas, an evil index,
The bagpipe-breasted ladies in the deadweed
Blew out the blood gauze through the wound of manwax.

VII

Now stamp the Lord's Prayer on a grain of rice,
A Bible-leaved of all the written woods
Strip to this tree: a rocking alphabet,
Genesis in the root, the scarecrow word,
And one light's language in the book of trees.
Doom on deniers at the wind-turned statement.
Time's tune my ladies with the teats of music,
The scaled sea-sawers, fix in a naked sponge
Who sucks the bell-voiced Adam out of magic,
Time, milk, and magic, from the world beginning.
Time is the tune my ladies lend their heartbreak,

From bald pavilions and the house of bread
Time tracks the sound of shape on man and cloud,
On rose and icicle the ringing handprint.

VIII

This was the crucifixion on the mountain,
Time's nerve in vinegar, the gallow grave
As tarred with blood as the bright thorns I wept;
The world's my wound, God's Mary in her grief,
Bent like three trees and bird-papped through her shift,
With pins for teardrops is the long wound's woman.
This was the sky, Jack Christ, each minstrel angle
Drove in the heaven-driven of the nails
Till the three-coloured rainbow from my nipples
From pole to pole leapt round the snail-waked world.
I by the tree of thieves, all glory's sawbones,
Unsex the skeleton this mountain minute,
And by this blowclock witness of the sun
Suffer the heaven's children through my heartbeat.

IX

From the oracular archives and the parchment,
Prophets and fibre kings in oil and letter,
The lamped calligrapher, the queen in splints,
Buckle to lint and cloth their natron footsteps,
Draw on the glove of prints, dead Cairo's henna
Pour like a halo on the caps and serpents.
This was the resurrection in the desert,
Death from a bandage, rants the mask of scholars
Gold on such features, and the linen spirit
Weds my long gentleman to dusts and furies;
With priest and pharaoh bed my gentle wound,
World in the sand, on the triangle landscape,
With stones of odyssey for ash and garland
And rivers of the dead around my neck.

X

Let the tale's sailor from a Christian voyage
Atlaswise hold half-way off the dummy bay
Time's ship-racked gospel on the globe I balance:
So shall winged harbours through the rockbirds' eyes
Spot the blown word, and on the seas I image
December's thorn screwed in a brow of holly.
Let the first Peter from a rainbow's quayrail
Ask the tall fish swept from the bible east,
What rhubarb man peeled in her foam-blue channel
Has sown a flying garden round that sea-ghost?
Green as beginning, let the garden diving
Soar, with its two bark towers, to that Day
When the worm builds with the gold straws of venom
My nest of mercies in the rude, red tree.

104

INCARNATE DEVIL

Incarnate devil in a talking snake,
The central plains of Asia in his garden,
In shaping-time the circle stung awake,
In shapes of sin forked out the bearded apple,
And God walked there who was a fiddling warden
And played down pardon from the heavens' hill.

When we were strangers to the guided seas,
A handmade moon half holy in a cloud,
The wisemen tell me that the garden gods
Twined good and evil on an eastern tree;
And when the moon rose windily it was
Black as the beast and paler than the cross.

We in our Eden knew the secret guardian
In sacred waters that no frost could harden,
And in the mighty mornings of the earth;
Hell in a horn of sulphur and the cloven myth,
All heaven in a midnight of the sun,
A serpent fiddled in the shaping-time.

105

HOLD HARD, THESE ANCIENT MINUTES IN THE CUCKOO'S MONTH

Hold hard, these ancient minutes in the cuckoo's month,
Under the lank, fourth folly on Glamorgan's hill,
As the green blooms ride upward, to the drive of time;
Time, in a folly's rider, like a county man
Over the vault of ridings with his hound at heel,
Drives forth my men, my children, from the hanging south.

Country, your sport is summer, and December's pools
By crane and water-tower by the seedy trees
Lie this fifth month unskated, and the birds have flown;
Hold hard, my country children in the world of tales,
The greenwood dying as the deer fall in their tracks,
This first and steepled season, to the summer's game.

And now the horns of England, in the sound of shape,
Summon your snowy horsemen, and the four-stringed hill,
Over the sea-gut loudening, sets a rock alive;
Hurdles and guns and railings, as the boulders heave,
Crack like a spring in a vice, bone breaking April,
Spill the lank folly's hunter and the hard-held hope.

Down fall four padding weathers on the scarlet lands,
Stalking my children's faces with a tail of blood,
Time, in a rider rising, from the harnessed valley;

Hold hard, my county darlings, for a hawk descends,
Golden Glamorgan straightens, to the falling birds.
Your sport is summer as the spring runs angrily.

FOSTER THE LIGHT

Foster the light nor veil the manshaped moon,
Nor weather winds that blow not down the bone,
But strip the twelve-winded marrow from his circle;
Master the night nor serve the snowman's brain
That shapes each bushy item of the air
Into a polestar pointed on an icicle.

Murmur of spring nor crush the cockerel's eggs,
Nor hammer back a season in the figs,
But graft these four-fruited ridings on your country;
Farmer in time of frost the burning leagues,
By red-eyed orchards sow the seeds of snow,
In your young years the vegetable century.

And father all nor fail the fly-lord's acre,
Nor sprout on owl-seed like a goblin-sucker,
But rail with your wizard's ribs the heart-shaped planet;
Of mortal voices to the ninnies' choir,
High lord esquire, speak up the singing cloud,
And pluck a mandrake music from the marrowroot.

Roll unmanly over this turning tuft,
O ring of seas, nor sorrow as I shift
From all my mortal lovers with a starboard smile;
Nor when my love lies in the cross-boned drift
Naked among the bow-and-arrow birds
Shall you turn cockwise on a tufted axle.
Who gave these seas their colour in a shape,

Shaped my clayfellow, and the heaven's ark
In time at flood filled with his coloured doubles;
O who is glory in the shapeless maps,
Now make the world of me as I have made
A merry manshape of your walking circle.

107

TODAY, THIS INSECT

Today, this insect, and the world I breathe,
Now that my symbols have outelbowed space,
Time at the city spectacles, and half
The dear, daft time I take to nudge the sentence,
In trust and tale have I divided sense,
Slapped down the guillotine, the blood-red double
Of head and tail made witnesses to this
Murder of Eden and green genesis.

The insect certain is the plague of fables.

This story's monster has a serpent caul,
Blind in the coil scrams round the blazing outline,
Measures his own length on the garden wall
And breaks his shell in the last shocked beginning;
A crocodile before the chrysalis,
Before the fall from love the flying heartbone,
Winged like a sabbath ass this children's piece
Uncredited blows Jericho on Eden.

The insect fable is the certain promise.

Death: death of Hamlet and the nightmare madmen,
An air-drawn windmill on a wooden horse,

John's beast, Job's patience, and the fibs of vision,
Greek in the Irish sea the ageless voice:
'Adam I love, my madmen's love is endless,
No tell-tale lover has an end more certain,
All legends' sweethearts on a tree of stories,
My cross of tales behind the fabulous curtain.'

108

THE SEED-AT-ZERO

The seed-at-zero shall not storm
That town of ghosts, the trodden womb
With her rampart to his tapping,
No god-in-hero tumble down
Like a tower on the town
Dumbly and divinely stumbling
Over the manwaging line.

The seed-at-zero shall not storm
That town of ghosts, the manwaged womb
With her rampart to his tapping,
No god-in-hero tumble down
Like a tower on the town
Dumbly and divinely leaping
Over the warbearing line.

Through the rampart of the sky
Shall the star-flanked seed be riddled,
Manna for the rumbling ground,
Quickening for the riddled sea;
Settled on a virgin stronghold

He shall grapple with the guard
And the keeper of the key.

Through the rampart of the sky
Shall the star-flanked seed be riddled,
Manna for the guarded ground,
Quickening for the virgin sea;
Settling on a riddled stronghold
He shall grapple with the guard
And the loser of the key.

May a humble village labour
And a continent deny?
A hemisphere may scold him
And a green inch be his bearer;
Let the hero seed find harbour,
Seaports by a drunken shore
Have their thirsty sailors hide him.

May a humble planet labour
And a continent deny?
A village green may scold him
And a high sphere be his bearer;
Let the hero seed find harbour,
Seaports by a thirsty shore
Have their drunken sailors hide him.

Man-in-seed, in seed-at-zero,
From the foreign fields of space,
Shall not thunder on the town
With a star-flanked garrison,
Nor the cannons of his kingdom
Shall the hero-in-tomorrow
Range on the sky-scraping place.

Man-in-seed, in seed-at-zero,
From the star-flanked fields of space,
Thunders on the foreign town
With a sand-bagged garrison,
Nor the cannons of his kingdom
Shall the hero-in-tomorrow
Range from the grave-groping place.

109

NOW

Now
Say nay,
Man dry man,
Dry lover mine
The deadrock base and blow the flowered anchor,
Should he, for centre sake, hop in the dust,
Forsake, the fool, the hardiness of anger.

Now
Say nay,
Sir no say,
Death to the yes,
The yes to death, the yesman and the answer,
Should he who split his children with a cure
Have brotherless his sister on the handsaw.

Now
Say nay,
No say sir
Yea the dead stir,
And this, nor this, is shade, the landed crow,
He lying low with ruin in his ear,
The cockerel's tide upcasting from the fire.

[127]

Now
Say nay,
So star fall,
So the ball fail,
So solve the mystic sun, the wife of light,
The sun that leaps on petals through a nought,
The come-a-cropper rider of the flower.

Now
Say nay
A fig for
The seal of fire,
Death hairy-heeled, and the tapped ghost in wood,
We make me mystic as the arm of air,
The two-a-vein, the foreskin, and the cloud.

110

THEN WAS MY NEOPHYTE

Then was my neophyte,
Child in white blood bent on its knees
Under the bell of rocks,
Ducked in the twelve, disciple seas
The winder of the water-clocks
Calls a green day and night.
My sea hermaphrodite,
Snail of man in His ship of fires
That burn the bitten decks,
Knew all His horrible desires
The climber of the water sex
Calls the green rock of light.

Who in these labyrinths,
This tidethread and the lane of scales,

Twine in a moon-blown shell,
Escapes to the flat cities' sails
Furled on the fishes' house and hell,
Nor falls to His green myths?
Stretch the salt photographs,
The landscape grief, love in His oils
Mirror from man to whale
That the green child see like a grail
Through veil and fin and fire and coil
Time on the canvas paths.

He films my vanity.
Shot in the wind, by tilted arcs,
Over the water come
Children from homes and children's parks
Who speak on a finger and thumb,
And the masked, headless boy.
His reels and mystery
The winder of the clockwise scene
Wound like a ball of lakes
Then threw on that tide-hoisted screen
Love's image till my heartbone breaks
By a dramatic sea.

Who kills my history?
The year-hedged row is lame with flint,
Blunt scythe and water blade.
'Who could snap off the shapeless print
From your tomorrow-treading shade
With oracle for eye?'
Time kills me terribly.
'Time shall not murder you,' He said,
'Nor the green nought be hurt;
Who could hack out your unsucked heart,
O green and unborn and undead?'
I saw time murder me.

IT IS THE SINNERS' DUST-TONGUED BELL

It is the sinners' dust-tongued bell claps me to churches
When, with his torch and hourglass, like a sulphur priest,
His beast heel cleft in a sandal,
Time marks a black aisle kindle from the brand of ashes,
Grief with dishevelled hands tear out the altar ghost
And a firewind kill the candle.

Over the choir minute I hear the hour chant:
Time's coral saint and the salt grief drown a foul sepulchre
And a whirlpool drives the prayerwheel;
Moonfall and sailing emperor, pale as their tide-print,
Hear by death's accident the clocked and dashed-down spire
Strike the sea hour through bellmetal.

There is loud and dark directly under the dumb flame,
Storm, snow, and fountain in the weather of fireworks,
Cathedral calm in the pulled house;
Grief with drenched book and candle christens the cherub time
From the emerald, still bell; and from the pacing weather-cock
The voice of bird on coral prays.

Forever it is a white child in the dark-skinned summer
Out of the font of bone and plants at that stone tocsin
Scales the blue wall of spirits;
From blank and leaking winter sails the child in colour,
Shakes, in crabbed burial shawl, by sorcerer's insect woken,
Ding dong from the mute turrets.

I mean by time the cast and curfew rascal of our marriage,
At nightbreak born in the fat side, from an animal bed
In a holy room in a wave;
And all love's sinners in sweet cloth kneel to a hyleg image,

Nutmeg, civet, and sea-parsley serve the plagued groom and bride
Who have brought forth the urchin grief.

I MAKE THIS IN A WARRING ABSENCE

I make this in a warring absence when
Each ancient, stone-necked minute of love's season
Harbours my anchored tongue, slips the quaystone,
When, praise is blessed, her pride in mast and fountain
Sailed and set dazzling by the handshaped ocean,
In that proud sailing tree with branches driven
Through the last vault and vegetable groyne,
And this weak house to marrow-columned heaven,

Is corner-cast, breath's rag, scrawled weed, a vain
And opium head, crow stalk, puffed, cut, and blown,
Or like the tide-looped breastknot reefed again
Or rent ancestrally the roped sea-hymen,
And, pride is last, is like a child alone
By magnet winds to her blind mother drawn,
Bread and milk mansion in a toothless town.

She makes for me a nettle's innocence
And a silk pigeon's guilt in her proud absence,
In the molested rocks the shell of virgins,
The frank, closed pearl, the sea-girls' lineaments
Glint in the staved and siren-printed caverns,
Is maiden in the shameful oak, omens
Whalebed and bulldance, the gold bush of lions,
Proud as a sucked stone and huge as sandgrains.

These are her contraries: the beast who follows
With priest's grave foot and hand of five assassins

Her molten flight up cinder-nesting columns,
Calls the starved fire herd, is cast in ice,
Lost in a limp-treed and uneating silence,
Who scales a hailing hill in her cold flintsteps
Falls on a ring of summers and locked noons.

I make a weapon of an ass's skeleton
And walk the warring sands by the dead town,
Cudgel great air, wreck east, and topple sundown,
Storm her sped heart, hang with beheaded veins
Its wringing shell, and let her eyelids fasten.
Destruction, picked by birds, brays through the jaw-bone
And, for that murder's sake, dark with contagion
Like an approaching wave I sprawl to ruin.

Ruin, the room of errors, one rood dropped
Down the stacked sea and water-pillared shade,
Weighed in rock shroud, is my proud pyramid;
Where, wound in emerald linen and sharp wind,
The hero's head lies scraped of every legend,
Comes love's anatomist with sun-gloved hand
Who picks the live heart on a diamond.

'His mother's womb had a tongue that lapped up mud,'
Cried the topless, inchtaped lips from hank and hood
In that bright anchorground where I lay linened,
'A lizard darting with black venom's thread
Doubled, to fork him back, through the lockjaw bed
And the breath-white, curtained mouth of seed.'
'See,' drummed the taut masks, 'how the dead ascend:
In the groin's endless coil a man is tangled.'

These once-blind eyes have breathed a wind of visions,
The cauldron's root through this once-rindless hand

[132]

Fumed like a tree, and tossed a burning bird;
With loud, torn tooth and tail and cobweb drum
The crumpled packs fled past this ghost in bloom,
And, mild as pardon from a cloud of pride,
The terrible world my brother bares his skin.

Now in the cloud's big breast lie quiet countries,
Delivered seas my love from her proud place
Walks with no wound, nor lightning in her face,
A calm wind blows that raised the trees like hair
Once where the soft snow's blood was turned to ice.
And though my love pulls the pale, nippled air,
Prides of tomorrow suckling in her eyes,
Yet this I make in a forgiving presence.

113

O MAKE ME A MASK

O make me a mask and a wall to shut from your spies
Of the sharp, enamelled eyes and the spectacled claws
Rape and rebellion in the nurseries of my face,
Gag of a dumbstruck tree to block from bare enemies
The bayonet tongue in this undefended prayerpiece,
The present mouth, and the sweetly blown trumpet of lies,
Shaped in old armour and oak the countenance of a dunce
To shield the glistening brain and blunt the examiners,
And a tear-stained widower grief drooped from the lashes
To veil belladonna and let the dry eyes perceive
Others betray the lamenting lies of their losses
By the curve of the nude mouth or the laugh up the sleeve.

NOT FROM THIS ANGER

Not from this anger, anticlimax after
Refusal struck her loin and the lame flower
Bent like a beast to lap the singular floods
In a land strapped by hunger
Shall she receive a bellyful of weeds
And bear those tendril hands I touch across
The agonized, two seas.

Behind my head a square of sky sags over
The circular smile tossed from lover to lover
And the golden ball spins out of the skies;
Not from this anger after
Refusal struck like a bell under water
Shall her smile breed that mouth, behind the mirror,
That burns along my eyes.

HOW SHALL MY ANIMAL

How shall my animal
Whose wizard shape I trace in the cavernous skull,
Vessel of abscesses and exultation's shell,
Endure burial under the spelling wall,
The invoked, shrouding veil at the cap of the face,
Who should be furious,
Drunk as a vineyard snail, flailed like an octopus,
Roaring, crawling, quarrel
With the outside weathers,
The natural circle of the discovered skies
Draw down to its weird eyes?

How shall it magnetize,
Towards the studded male in a bent, midnight blaze
That melts the lionhead's heel and horseshoe of the heart,
A brute land in the cool top of the country days
To trot with a loud mate the haybeds of a mile,
Love and labour and kill
In quick, sweet, cruel light till the locked ground sprout out,
The black, burst sea rejoice,
The bowels turn turtle,
Claw of the crabbed veins squeeze from each red particle
The parched and raging voice?

Fishermen of mermen
Creep and harp on the tide, sinking their charmed, bent pin
With bridebait of gold bread, I with a living skein,
Tongue and ear in the thread, angle the temple-bound
Curl-locked and animal cavepools of spells and bone,
Trace out a tentacle,
Nailed with an open eye, in the bowl of wounds and weed
To clasp my fury on ground
And clap its great blood down;
Never shall beast be born to atlas the few seas
Or poise the day on a horn.

Sigh long, clay cold, lie shorn,
Cast high, stunned on gilled stone; sly scissors ground in frost
Clack through the thicket of strength, love hewn in pillars drops
With carved bird, saint, and sun, the wrackspiked maiden mouth
Lops, as a bush plumed with flames, the rant of the fierce eye,
Clips short the gesture of breath.
Die in red feathers when the flying heaven's cut,
And roll with the knocked earth:
Lie dry, rest robbed, my beast.
You have kicked from a dark den, leaped up the whinnying light,
And dug your grave in my breast.

AFTER THE FUNERAL

(In memory of Ann Jones)

After the funeral, mule praises, brays,
Windshake of sailshaped ears, muffle-toed tap
Tap happily of one peg in the thick
Grave's foot, blinds down the lids, the teeth in black,
The spittled eyes, the salt ponds in the sleeves,
Morning smack of the spade that wakes up sleep,
Shakes a desolate boy who slits his throat
In the dark of the coffin and sheds dry leaves,
That breaks one bone to light with a judgment clout,
After the feast of tear-stuffed time and thistles
In a room with a stuffed fox and a stale fern,
I stand, for this memorial's sake, alone
In the snivelling hours with dead, humped Ann
Whose hooded, fountain heart once fell in puddles
Round the parched worlds of Wales and drowned each sun
(Though this for her is a monstrous image blindly
Magnified out of praise; her death was a still drop;
She would not have me sinking in the holy
Flood of her heart's fame; she would lie dumb and deep
And need no druid of her broken body).
But I, Ann's bard on a raised hearth, call all
The seas to service that her wood-tongued virtue
Babble like a bellbuoy over the hymning heads,
Bow down the walls of the ferned and foxy woods
That her love sing and swing through a brown chapel,
Bless her bent spirit with four, crossing birds.
Her flesh was meek as milk, but this skyward statue
With the wild breast and blessed and giant skull
Is carved from her in a room with a wet window
In a fiercely mourning house in a crooked year.
I know her scrubbed and sour humble hands

Lie with religion in their cramp, her threadbare
Whisper in a damp word, her wits drilled hollow,
Her fist of a face died clenched on a round pain;
And sculptured Ann is seventy years of stone.
These cloud-sopped, marble hands, this monumental
Argument of the hewn voice, gesture and psalm,
Storm me forever over her grave until
The stuffed lung of the fox twitch and cry Love
And the strutting fern lay seeds on the black sill.

117

O CHATTERTON

O Chatterton and others in the attic
Linked in one gas bracket
Taking Jeyes' fluid as narcotic;
Drink from the earth's teats,
Life neat's a better poison than in bottle,
A better venom seethes in spittle
Than one could probe out of a serpent's guts;
Each new sensation emits
A new vinegar;
Be a regular
Fellow with saw at the jugular.
On giddy nights when slap on the moon's mask
A madman with a brush has slapped a face
I pick a stick of celery from the valley
I find a tripper's knicker in the gully
And take another nibble at my flask.
What meaning, voices, in the straight-ruled grass,
Meaning in hot sock soil? A little cuss
Can't read sense in the rain that willynilly
Soaks to the vest old dominies and drunks.
Dissect that statement, voices, on the slabs.

Love's a decision of 3 nerves
And Up and Down love's questions ask;
On giddy nights I slap a few drunk curves
Slap on the drunk moon's mask.
Rape gulp and be marry, he also serves
Who only drinks his profits
And would a-wooing go around the graves.
Celibate I sit and see
Women figures round my cell,
Women figures on the wall
Point their little breasts at me;
I must wait for a woman's smile
Not in the sun but in the dark;
The two words stallion and sterile
Stand in a question mark.
The smiling woman is a mad story,
Wipe it away, wipe a crumb
From the preacher's table.
I offer you women, not woman,
A home and a dowry:
3 little lusts shall your dowry be,
And your home in a centaur's stable.

118

WHEN ALL MY FIVE AND COUNTRY SENSES SEE

When all my five and country senses see,
The fingers will forget green thumbs and mark
How, through the halfmoon's vegetable eye,
Husk of young stars and handfull zodiac,
Love in the frost is pared and wintered by,
The whispering ears will watch love drummed away
Down breeze and shell to a discordant beach,

And, lashed to syllables, the lynx tongue cry
That her fond wounds are mended bitterly.
My nostrils see her breath burn like a bush.

My one and noble heart has witnesses
In all love's countries, that will grope awake;
And when blind sleep drops on the spying senses,
The heart is sensual, though five eyes break.

119

THE TOMBSTONE TOLD WHEN SHE DIED

The tombstone told when she died.
Her two surnames stopped me still.
A virgin married at rest.
She married in this pouring place,
That I struck one day by luck,
Before I heard in my mother's side
Or saw in the looking-glass shell
The rain through her cold heart speak
And the sun killed in her face.
More the thick stone cannot tell.

Before she lay on a stranger's bed
With a hand plunged through her hair,
Or that rainy tongue beat back
Through the devilish years and innocent deaths
To the room of a secret child,
Among men later I heard it said
She cried her white-dressed limbs were bare
And her red lips were kissed black,
She wept in her pain and made mouths,
Talked and tore though her eyes smiled.

I who saw in a hurried film
Death and this mad heroine
Meet once on a mortal wall,
Heard her speak through the chipped beak
Of the stone bird guarding her:
I died before bedtime came
But my womb was bellowing
And I felt with my bare fall
A blazing red harsh head tear up
And the dear floods of his hair.

120

ON NO WORK OF WORDS

On no work of words now for three lean months in the bloody
Belly of the rich year and the big purse of my body
I bitterly take to task my poverty and craft:

To take to give is all, return what is hungrily given
Puffing the pounds of manna up through the dew to heaven,
The lovely gift of the gab bangs back on a blind shaft.

To lift to leave from the treasures of man is pleasing death
That will rake at last all currencies of the marked breath
And count the taken, forsaken mysteries in a bad dark.

To surrender now is to pay the expensive ogre twice.
Ancient woods of my blood, dash down to the nut of the seas
If I take to burn or return this world which is each man's work.

I, THE FIRST NAMED

I, the first named, am the ghost of this sir and Christian friend
Who writes these words I write in a still room in a spellsoaked
  house:
I am the ghost in this house that is filled with the tongue and eyes
Of a lack-a-head ghost I fear to the anonymous end.

A SAINT ABOUT TO FALL

A saint about to fall,
The stained flats of heaven hit and razed
To the kissed kite hems of his shawl,
On the last street wave praised
The unwinding, song by rock,
Of the woven wall
Of his father's house in the sands,
The vanishing of the musical ship-work and the chucked bells,
The wound-down cough of the blood-counting clock
Behind a face of hands,
On the angelic etna of the last whirring featherlands,
Wind-heeled foot in the hole of a fireball,
Hymned his shrivelling flock,
On the last rick's tip by spilled wine-wells
Sang heaven hungry and the quick
Cut Christbread spitting vinegar and all
The mazes of his praise and envious tongue were worked in flames
  and shells.

Glory cracked like a flea.
The sun-leaved holy candlewoods

Drivelled down to one singeing tree
With a stub of black buds,
The sweet, fish-gilled boats bringing blood
Lurched through a scuttled sea
With a hold of leeches and straws,
Heaven fell with his fall and one crocked bell beat the left air.
O wake in me in my house in the mud
Of the crotch of the squawking shores,
Flicked from the carbolic city puzzle in a bed of sores
The scudding base of the familiar sky,
The lofty roots of the clouds.
From an odd room in a split house stare,
Milk in your mouth, at the sour floods
That bury the sweet street slowly, see
The skull of the earth is barbed with a war of burning brains and
    hair.

Strike in the time-bomb town,
Raise the live rafters of the eardrum,
Throw your fear a parcel of stone
Through the dark asylum,
Lapped among herods wail
As their blade marches in
That the eyes are already murdered,
The stocked heart is forced, and agony has another mouth to feed.
O wake to see, after a noble fall,
The old mud hatch again, the horrid
Woe drip from the dishrag hands and the pressed sponge of the
    forehead,
The breath draw back like a bolt through white oil
And a stranger enter like iron.
Cry joy that this witchlike midwife second
Bullies into rough seas you so gentle
And makes with a flick of the thumb and sun
A thundering bullring of your silent and girl-circled island.

TWENTY-FOUR YEARS

Twenty-four years remind the tears of my eyes.
(Bury the dead for fear that they walk to the grave in labour.)
In the groin of the natural doorway I crouched like a tailor
Sewing a shroud for a journey
By the light of the meat-eating sun.
Dressed to die, the sensual strut begun,
With my red veins full of money,
In the final direction of the elementary town
I advance for as long as forever is.

THE MOLLS

I found them lying on the floor,
Male shapes, girl-lipped, but clad like boys:
Night after night their hands implore
Emetic Percies for their joys.

They retch into my secret night
With stale and terrifying camp
And offer as the last delight
A crude, unhappy, anal cramp.

Gently they sigh to my behind
Wilde words, all buttered, badly bred,
And when I dream of them I find
Peacockstain's poems on my bed.

ONCE IT WAS THE COLOUR OF SAYING

Once it was the colour of saying
Soaked my table the uglier side of a hill
With a capsized field where a school sat still
And a black and white patch of girls grew playing;
The gentle seaslides of saying I must undo
That all the charmingly drowned arise to cockcrow and kill.
When I whistled with mitching boys through a reservoir park
Where at night we stoned the cold and cuckoo
Lovers in the dirt of their leafy beds,
The shade of their trees was a word of many shades
And a lamp of lightning for the poor in the dark;
Now my saying shall be my undoing,
And every stone I wind off like a reel.

BECAUSE THE PLEASURE-BIRD WHISTLES

Because the pleasure-bird whistles after the hot wires,
Shall the blind horse sing sweeter?
Convenient bird and beast lie lodged to suffer
The supper and knives of a mood.
In the sniffed and poured snow on the tip of the tongue of the year
That clouts the spittle like bubbles with broken rooms,
An enamoured man alone by the twigs of his eyes, two fires,
Camped in the drug-white shower of nerves and food,
Savours the lick of the times through a deadly wood of hair
In a wind that plucked a goose,
Nor ever, as the wild tongue breaks its tombs,
Rounds to look at the red, wagged root.
Because there stands, one story out of the bum city,

That frozen wife whose juices drift like a fixed sea
Secretly in statuary,
Shall I, struck on the hot and rocking street,
Not spin to stare at an old year
Toppling and burning in the muddle of towers and galleries
Like the mauled pictures of boys?
The salt person and blasted place
I furnish with the meat of a fable;
If the dead starve, their stomachs turn to tumble
An upright man in the antipodes
Or spray-based and rock-chested sea:
Over the past table I repeat this present grace.

127

'IF MY HEAD HURT A HAIR'S FOOT'

'If my head hurt a hair's foot
Pack back the downed bone. If the unpricked ball of my breath
Bump on a spout let the bubbles jump out.
Sooner drop with the worm of the ropes round my throat
Than bully ill love in the clouted scene.

'All game phrases fit your ring of a cockfight:
I'll comb the snared woods with a glove on a lamp,
Peck, sprint, dance on fountains and duck time
Before I rush in a crouch the ghost with a hammer, air,
Strike light, and bloody a loud room.

'If my bunched, monkey coming is cruel
Rage me back to the making house. My hand unravel
When you sew the deep door. The bed is a cross place.
Bend, if my journey ache, direction like an arc or make
A limp and riderless shape to leap nine thinning months.'

[145]

'No. Not for Christ's dazzling bed
Or a nacreous sleep among soft particles and charms
My dear would I change my tears or your iron head.
Thrust, my daughter or son, to escape, there is none, none, none,
Nor when all ponderous heaven's host of waters breaks.

'Now to awake husked of gestures and my joy like a cave
To the anguish and carrion, to the infant forever unfree,
O my lost love bounced from a good home;
The grain that hurries this way from the rim of the grave
Has a voice and a house, and there and here you must couch and
    cry.

'Rest beyond choice in the dust-appointed grain,
At the breast stored with seas. No return
Through the waves of the fat streets nor the skeleton's thin ways.
The grave and my calm body are shut to your coming as stone,
And the endless beginning of prodigies suffers open.'

128

TO OTHERS THAN YOU

Friend by enemy I call you out.

You with a bad coin in your socket,
You my friend there with a winning air
Who palmed the lie on me when you looked
Brassily at my shyest secret,
Enticed with twinkling bits of the eye
Till the sweet tooth of my love bit dry,
Rasped at last, and I stumbled and sucked,
Whom now I conjure to stand as thief
In the memory worked by mirrors,
With unforgettably smiling act,

Quickness of hand in the velvet glove
And my whole heart under your hammer,
Were once such a creature, so gay and frank
A desireless familiar
I never thought to utter or think
While you displaced a truth in the air,

That though I loved them for their faults
As much as for their good,
My friends were enemies on stilts
With their heads in a cunning cloud.

129

UNLUCKILY FOR A DEATH

Unluckily for a death
Waiting with phoenix under
The pyre yet to be lighted of my sins and days,
And for the woman in shades
Saint carved and sensual among the scudding
Dead and gone, dedicate forever to my self
Though the brawl of the kiss has not occurred
On the clay cold mouth, on the fire
Branded forehead, that could bind
Her constant, nor the winds of love broken wide
To the wind the choir and cloister
Of the wintry nunnery of the order of lust
Beneath my life, that sighs for the seducer's coming
In the sun strokes of summer,

Loving on this sea banged guilt
My holy lucky body
Under the cloud against love is caught and held and kissed

In the mill of the midst
Of the descending day, the dark our folly
Cut to the still star in the order of the quick
But blessed by such heroic hosts in your every
Inch and glance that the wound
Is certain god, and the ceremony of souls
Is celebrated there, and communion between suns.
Never shall my self chant
About the saint in shades while the endless breviary
Turns of your prayed flesh, nor shall I shoo the bird below me:
The death biding two lie lonely.

I see the tigron in tears
In the androgynous dark,
His striped and noon maned tribe striding to holocaust,
The she mules bear their minotaurs,
The duck-billed platypus broody in a milk of birds.
I see the wanting nun saint carved in a garb
Of shades, symbol of desire beyond my hours
And guilts, great crotch and giant
Continence. I see the unfired phoenix, herald
And heaven crier, arrow now of aspiring
And the renouncing of islands.
All love but for the full assemblage in flower
Of the living flesh is monstrous or immortal,
And the grave its daughters.

Love, my fate got luckily,
Teaches with no telling
That the phoenix' bid for heaven and the desire after
Death in the carved nunnery
Both shall fail if I bow not to your blessing
Nor walk in the cool of your mortal garden
With immortality at my side like Christ the sky.
This I know from the native
Tongue of your translating eyes. The young stars told me,

Hurling into beginning like Christ the child.
Lucklessly she must lie patient
And the vaulting bird be still. O my true love, hold me.
In your every inch and glance is the globe of genesis spun,
And the living earth your sons.

130

PAPER AND STICKS

Paper and sticks and shovel and match
Why won't the news of the old world catch
And the fire in a temper start

Once I had a rich boy for myself
I loved his body and his navy blue wealth
And I lived in his purse and his heart

When in our bed I was tossing and turning
All I could see were his brown eyes burning
By the green of a one pound note

I talk to him as I clean the grate
O my dear it's never too late
To take me away as you whispered and wrote

I had a handsome and well-off boy
I'll share my money and we'll run for joy
With a bouncing and silver spooned kid

Sharp and shrill my silly tongue scratches
Words on the air as the fire catches
You never did and *he* never did.

WHEN I WOKE

When I woke, the town spoke.
Birds and clocks and cross bells
Dinned aside the coiling crowd,
The reptile profligates in a flame,
Spoilers and pokers of sleep,
The next-door sea dispelled
Frogs and satans and woman-luck,
While a man outside with a billhook,
Up to his head in his blood,
Cutting the morning off,
The warm-veined double of Time
And his scarving beard from a book,
Slashed down the last snake as though
It were a wand or subtle bough,
Its tongue peeled in the wrap of a leaf.

Every morning I make,
God in bed, good and bad,
After a water-face walk,
The death-stagged scatter-breath
Mammoth and sparrowfall
Everybody's earth.
Where birds ride like leaves and boats like ducks
I heard, this morning, waking,
Crossly out of the town noises
A voice in the erected air,
No prophet-progeny of mine,
Cry my sea town was breaking.
No Time, spoke the clocks, no God, rang the bells,
I drew the white sheet over the islands
And the coins on my eyelids sang like shells.

ONCE BELOW A TIME

I

Once below a time
When my pinned-around-the-spirit
Cut-to-measure flesh bit,
Suit for a serial sum
On the first of each hardship,
My paid-for slaved-for own too late
In love torn breeches and blistered jacket
On the snapping rims of the ashpit,
In grottoes I worked with birds,
Spiked with a mastiff collar,
Tasselled in cellar and snipping shop
Or decked on a cloud swallower,

Then swift from a bursting sea with bottlecork boats
And out-of-perspective sailors,
In common clay clothes disguised as scales,
As a he-god's paddling water skirts,
I astounded the sitting tailors,
I set back the clock faced tailors,
Then, bushily swanked in bear wig and tails,
Hopping hot leaved and feathered
From the kangaroo foot of the earth,
From the chill, silent centre
Trailing the frost bitten cloth,
Up through the lubber crust of Wales
I rocketed to astonish
The flashing needle rock of squatters,
The criers of Shabby and Shorten,
The famous stitch droppers.

II

My silly suit, hardly yet suffered for,
Around some coffin carrying
Birdman or told ghost I hung.
And the owl hood, the heel hider,
Claw fold and hole for the rotten
Head, deceived, I believed, my maker,

The cloud perched tailors' master with nerves for cotton.
On the old seas from stories, thrashing my wings,
Combing with antlers, Columbus on fire,
I was pierced by the idol tailor's eyes,
Glared through shark mask and navigating head,
Cold Nansen's beak on a boat full of gongs,

To the boy of common thread,
The bright pretender, the ridiculous sea dandy
With dry flesh and earth for adorning and bed.
It was sweet to drown in the readymade handy water
With my cherry capped dangler green as seaweed

Summoning a child's voice from a webfoot stone,
Never never oh never to regret the bugle I wore
On my cleaving arm as I blasted in a wave.
Now shown and mostly bare I would lie down,
Lie down, lie down and live
As quiet as a bone.

133

THERE WAS A SAVIOUR

There was a saviour
Rarer than radium,
Commoner than water, crueller than truth;
Children kept from the sun
Assembled at his tongue

To hear the golden note turn in a groove,
Prisoners of wishes locked in their eyes
In the jails and studies of his keyless smiles.

The voice of children says
From a lost wilderness
There was calm to be done in his safe unrest,
When hindering man hurt
Man, animal, or bird
We hid our fears in that murdering breath,
Silence, silence to do, when earth grew loud,
In lairs and asylums of the tremendous shout.

There was glory to hear
In the churches of his tears,
Under his downy arm you sighed as he struck,
O you who could not cry
On to the ground when a man died
Put a tear for joy in the unearthly flood
And laid your cheek against a cloud-formed shell:
Now in the dark there is only yourself and myself.

Two proud, blacked brothers cry,
Winter-locked side by side,
To this inhospitable hollow year,
O we who could not stir
One lean sigh when we heard
Greed on man beating near and fire neighbour
But wailed and nested in the sky-blue wall
Now break a giant tear for the little known fall,

For the drooping of homes
That did not nurse our bones,
Brave deaths of only ones but never found,
Now see, alone in us,
Our own true strangers' dust

Ride through the doors of our unentered house.
Exiled in us we arouse the soft,
Unclenched, armless, silk and rough love that breaks all rocks.

134

THE COUNTRYMAN'S RETURN

Embracing low-falutin
London (said the odd man in
A country pot, his hutch in
The fields, by a motherlike henrun)
With my fishtail hands and gently
Manuring popeye or
Swelling in flea-specked linen
The rankest of the city
I spent my unwasteable
Time among walking pintables
With sprung and padded shoulders,
Tomorrow's drunk club majors
Growing their wounds already,
The last war's professional
Unclaimed dead, girls from good homes
Studying the testicle
In communal crab flats
With the Sunflowers laid on,
Old paint-stained tumblers riding
On stools to a one man show down,
Gasketted and sirensuited
Bored and viciously waiting
Nightingales of the casualty stations
In the afternoon wasters
White feathering the living.

London's arches are falling
In, in Pedro's or Wendy's

With a silverfox farmer
Trying his hand at failing
Again, a collected poet
And some dismantled women,
Razor man and belly king,
I propped humanity's weight
Against the fruit machine,
Opened my breast and into
The spongebag let them all melt.
Zip once more for a traveller
With his goods under his eyes,
Another with hers under her belt,
The black man bleached to his tide
Mark, trumpet lipped and blackhead
Eyed, while the tears drag on the tail,
The weighing-scales, of my hand.
Then into blind streets I swam
Alone with my bouncing bag,
Too full to bow to the dim
Moon with a relation's face
Or lift my hat to unseen
Brothers dodging through the fog
The affectionate pickpocket
And childish, snivelling queen.

Beggars, robbers, inveiglers,
Voices from manholes and drains,
Maternal short time pieces,
Octopuses in doorways,
Dark inviters to keyholes
And evenings with great danes,
Bedsitting girls on the beat
With nothing for the metre,
Others whose single beds hold two
Only to make two ends meet,

All the hypnotised city's
Insidious procession
Hawking for money and pity
Among the hardly possessed.
And I in the wanting sway
Caught among never enough
Conjured me to resemble
A singing Walt from the mower
And jerrystone trim villas
Of the upper of the lower half,
Beardlessly wagging in Dean Street,
Blessing and counting the bustling
Twolegged handbagged sparrows,
Flogging into the porches
My cavernous, featherbed self.

Cut. Cut the crushed streets, leaving
A hole of errands and shades;
Plug the paper-blowing tubes;
Emasculate the seedy clocks;
Rub off the scrawl of prints on
Body and air and building;
Branch and leaf the birdless roofs;
Faces of melting visions,
Magdalene prostitution,
Glamour of the bloodily bowed,
Exaltation of the blind,
That sin-embracing dripper of fun
Sweep away like a cream cloud;
Bury all rubbish and love signs
Of my week in the dirtbox
In this anachronistic scene
Where sitting in clean linen
In a hutch in a cowpatched glen
Now I delight, I suppose, in

The countryman's return
And count by birds' eggs and leaves
The rusticating minutes,
The wasteful hushes among trees.
And O to cut the green field, leaving
One rich street with hunger in it.

135

INTO HER LYING DOWN HEAD

I

Into her lying down head
His enemies entered bed,
Under the encumbered eyelid,
Through the rippled drum of the hair-buried ear;
And Noah's rekindled now unkind dove
Flew man-bearing there.
Last night in a raping wave
Whales unreined from the green grave
In fountains of origin gave up their love,
Along her innocence glided
Juan aflame and savagely young King Lear,
Queen Catherine howling bare
And Samson drowned in his hair,
The colossal intimacies of silent
Once seen strangers or shades on a stair;
There the dark blade and wanton sighing her down
To a haycock couch and the scythes of his arms
Rode and whistled a hundred times
Before the crowing morning climbed;
Man was the burning England she was sleep-walking, and the
enamouring island
Made her limbs blind by luminous charms,
Sleep to a newborn sleep in a swaddling loin-leaf stroked and sang
And his runaway beloved childlike laid in the acorned sand.

[157]

II

There where a numberless tongue
Wound their room with a male moan,
His faith around her flew undone
And darkness hung the walls with baskets of snakes,
A furnace-nostrilled column-membered
Super-or-near man
Resembling to her dulled sense
The thief of adolescence,
Early imaginary half remembered
Oceanic lover alone
Jealousy cannot forget for all her sakes,
Made his bad bed in her good
Night, and enjoyed as he would.
Crying, white gowned, from the middle moonlit stages
Out to the tiered and hearing tide,
Close and far she announced the theft of the heart
In the taken body at many ages,
Trespasser and broken bride
Celebrating at her side
All blood-signed assailings and vanished marriages in which he
had no lovely part
Nor could share, for his pride, to the least
Mutter and foul wingbeat of the solemnizing nightpriest
Her holy unholy hours with the always anonymous beast.

III

Two sand grains together in bed,
Head to heaven-circling head,
Singly lie with the whole wide shore,
The covering sea their nightfall with no names;
And out of every domed and soil-based shell
One voice in chains declaims
The female, deadly, and male
Libidinous betrayal,

Golden dissolving under the water veil.
     A she bird sleeping brittle by
Her lover's wings that fold to-morrow's flight,
          Within the nested treefork
          Sings to the treading hawk
Carrion, paradise, chirrup my bright yolk.
     A blade of grass longs with the meadow,
A stone lies lost and locked in the lark-high hill.
Open as to the air to the naked shadow
          O she lies alone and still,
          Innocent between two wars,
With the incestuous secret brother in the seconds to perpetuate
     the stars,
     A man torn up mourns in the sole night.
And the second comers, the severers, the enemies from the deep
Forgotten dark, rest their pulse and bury their dead in her
     faithless sleep.

136

REQUEST TO LEDA

(HOMAGE TO WILLIAM EMPSON)

Not your winged lust but his must now change suit.
The harp-waked Casanova rakes no range.
The worm is (pin-point) rational in the fruit.

Not girl for bird (gourd being man) breaks root.
Taking no plume for index in love's change
Not your winged lust but his must now change suit.

Desire is phosphorus: the chemic bruit
Lust bears like volts, who'll amplify, and strange
The worm is (pin-point) rational in the fruit.

DEATHS AND ENTRANCES

On almost the incendiary eve
　　Of several near deaths,
When one at the great least of your best loved
　　And always known must leave
Lions and fires of his flying breath,
　　Of your immortal friends
Who'd raise the organs of the counted dust
　　To shoot and sing your praise,
One who called deepest down shall hold his peace
　　That cannot sink or cease
　　Endlessly to his wound
In many married London's estranging grief.

On almost the incendiary eve
　　When at your lips and keys,
Locking, unlocking, the murdered strangers weave,
　　One who is most unknown,
Your polestar neighbour, sun of another street,
　　Will dive up to his tears.
He'll bathe his raining blood in the male sea
　　Who strode for your own dead
And wind his globe out of your water thread
　　And load the throats of shells
　　With every cry since light
Flashed first across his thunderclapping eyes.

On almost the incendiary eve
　　Of deaths and entrances,
When near and strange wounded on London's waves
　　Have sought your single grave,
One enemy, of many, who knows well
　　Your heart is luminous

[　160　]

In the watched dark, quivering through locks and caves,
  Will pull the thunderbolts
To shut the sun, plunge, mount your darkened keys
  And sear just riders back,
    Until that one loved least
Looms the last Samson of your zodiac.

138

ON A WEDDING ANNIVERSARY

The sky is torn across
This ragged anniversary of two
Who moved for three years in tune
Down the long walks of their vows.

Now their love lies a loss
And Love and his patients roar on a chain;
From every true or crater
Carrying cloud, Death strikes their house.

Too late in the wrong rain
They come together whom their love parted:
The windows pour into their heart
And the doors burn in their brain.

139

BALLAD OF THE LONG-LEGGED BAIT

The bows glided down, and the coast
Blackened with birds took a last look
At his thrashing hair and whale-blue eye;
The trodden town rang its cobbles for luck.

Then good-bye to the fishermanned
Boat with its anchor free and fast
As a bird hooking over the sea,
High and dry by the top of the mast,

Whispered the affectionate sand
And the bulwarks of the dazzled quay.
For my sake sail, and never look back,
Said the looking land.

Sails drank the wind, and white as milk
He sped into the drinking dark;
The sun shipwrecked west on a pearl
And the moon swam out of its hulk.

Funnels and masts went by in a whirl.
Good-bye to the man on the sea-legged deck
To the gold gut that sings on his reel
To the bait that stalked out of the sack,

For we saw him throw to the swift flood
A girl alive with his hooks through her lips;
All the fishes were rayed in blood,
Said the dwindling ships.

Good-bye to chimneys and funnels,
Old wives that spin in the smoke,
He was blind to the eyes of candles
In the praying windows of waves

But heard his bait buck in the wake
And tussle in a shoal of loves.
Now cast down your rod, for the whole
Of the sea is hilly with whales,

She longs among horses and angels,
The rainbow-fish bend in her joys,
Floated the lost cathedral
Chimes of the rocked buoys.

Where the anchor rode like a gull
Miles over the moonstruck boat
A squall of birds bellowed and fell,
A cloud blew the rain from its throat;

He saw the storm smoke out to kill
With fuming bows and ram of ice,
Fire on starlight, rake Jesu's stream;
And nothing shone on the water's face

But the oil and bubble of the moon,
Plunging and piercing in his course
The lured fish under the foam
Witnessed with a kiss.

Whales in the wake like capes and Alps
Quaked the sick sea and snouted deep,
Deep the great bushed bait with raining lips
Slipped the fins of those humpbacked tons

And fled their love in a weaving dip.
Oh, Jericho was falling in their lungs!
She nipped and dived in the nick of love,
Spun on a spout like a long-legged ball

Till every beast blared down in a swerve
Till every turtle crushed from his shell
Till every bone in the rushing grave
Rose and crowed and fell!

Good luck to the hand on the rod,
There is thunder under its thumbs;
Gold gut is a lightning thread,
His fiery reel sings off its flames,

The whirled boat in the burn of his blood
Is crying from nets to knives,
Oh the shearwater birds and their boatsized brood
Oh the bulls of Biscay and their calves

Are making under the green, laid veil
The long-legged beautiful bait their wives.
Break the black news and paint on a sail
Huge weddings in the waves,

Over the wakeward-flashing spray
Over the gardens of the floor
Clash out the mounting dolphin's day,
My mast is a bell-spire,

Strike and smoothe, for my decks are drums,
Sing through the water-spoken prow
The octopus walking into her limbs
The polar eagle with his tread of snow.

From salt-lipped beak to the kick of the stern
Sing how the seal has kissed her dead!
The long, laid minute's bride drifts on
Old in her cruel bed.

Over the graveyard in the water
Mountains and galleries beneath
Nightingale and hyena
Rejoicing for that drifting death

Sing and howl through sand and anemone
Valley and sahara in a shell,
Oh all the wanting flesh his enemy
Thrown to the sea in the shell of a girl

Is old as water and plain as an eel;
Always good-bye to the long-legged bread
Scattered in the paths of his heels
For the salty birds fluttered and fed

And the tall grains foamed in their bills;
Always good-bye to the fires of the face,
For the crab-backed dead on the sea-bed rose
And scuttled over her eyes,

The blind, clawed stare is cold as sleet.
The tempter under the eyelid
Who shows to the selves asleep
Mast-high moon-white women naked

Walking in wishes and lovely for shame
Is dumb and gone with his flame of brides.
Susannah's drowned in the bearded stream
And no-one stirs at Sheba's side

But the hungry kings of the tides;
Sin who had a woman's shape
Sleeps till Silence blows on a cloud
And all the lifted waters walk and leap.

Lucifer that bird's dropping
Out of the sides of the north
Has melted away and is lost
Is always lost in her vaulted breath,

Venus lies star-struck in her wound
And the sensual ruins make
Seasons over the liquid world,
White springs in the dark.

Always good-bye, cried the voices through the shell,
Good-bye always for the flesh is cast
And the fisherman winds his reel
With no more desire than a ghost.

Always good luck, praised the finned in the feather
Bird after dark and the laughing fish
As the sails drank up the hail of thunder
And the long-tailed lightning lit his catch.

The boat swims into the six-year weather,
A wind throws a shadow and it freezes fast.
See what the gold gut drags from under
Mountains and galleries to the crest!

See what clings to hair and skull
As the boat skims on with drinking wings!
The statues of great rain stand still,
And the flakes fall like hills.

Sing and strike his heavy haul
Toppling up the boatside in a snow of light!
His decks are drenched with miracles.
Oh miracle of fishes! The long dead bite!

Out of the urn the size of a man
Out of the room the weight of his trouble
Out of the house that holds a town
In the continent of a fossil

One by one in dust and shawl,
Dry as echoes and insect-faced,
His fathers cling to the hand of the girl
And the dead hand leads the past,

Leads them as children and as air
On to the blindly tossing tops;
The centuries throw back their hair
And the old men sing from newborn lips:

Time is bearing another son.
Kill Time! She turns in her pain!
The oak is felled in the acorn
And the hawk in the egg kills the wren.

He who blew the great fire in
And died on a hiss of flames
Or walked on the earth in the evening
Counting the denials of the grains

Clings to her drifting hair, and climbs;
And he who taught their lips to sing
Weeps like the risen sun among
The liquid choirs of his tribes.

The rod bends low, divining land,
And through the sundered water crawls
A garden holding to her hand
With birds and animals

With men and women and waterfalls
Trees cool and dry in the whirlpool of ships
And stunned and still on the green, laid veil
Sand with legends in its virgin laps

And prophets loud on the burned dunes;
Insects and valleys hold her thighs hard,
Time and places grip her breast bone,
She is breaking with seasons and clouds;

Round her trailed wrist fresh water weaves,
With moving fish and rounded stones
Up and down the greater waves
A separate river breathes and runs;

Strike and sing his catch of fields
For the surge is sown with barley,
The cattle graze on the covered foam,
The hills have footed the waves away,

With wild sea fillies and soaking bridles
With salty colts and gales in their limbs
All the horses of his haul of miracles
Gallop through the arched, green farms,

Trot and gallop with gulls upon them
And thunderbolts in their manes.
O Rome and Sodom To-morrow and London
The country tide is cobbled with towns,

And steeples pierce the cloud on her shoulder
And the streets that the fisherman combed
When his long-legged flesh was a wind on fire
And his loin was a hunting flame

Coil from the thoroughfares of her hair
And terribly lead him home alive
Lead her prodigal home to his terror,
The furious ox-killing house of love.

Down, down, down, under the ground,
Under the floating villages,
Turns the moon-chained and water-wound
Metropolis of fishes,

There is nothing left of the sea but its sound,
Under the earth the loud sea walks,
In deathbeds of orchards the boat dies down
And the bait is drowned among hayricks,

Land, land, land, nothing remains
Of the pacing, famous sea but its speech,
And into its talkative seven tombs
The anchor dives through the floors of a church.

Good-bye, good luck, struck the sun and the moon,
To the fisherman lost on the land.
He stands alone at the door of his home,
With his long-legged heart in his hand.

140

LOVE IN THE ASYLUM

A stranger has come
To share my room in the house not right in the head,
A girl mad as birds

Bolting the night of the door with her arm her plume.
Strait in the mazed bed
She deludes the heaven-proof house with entering clouds

Yet she deludes with walking the nightmarish room,
At large as the dead,
Or rides the imagined oceans of the male wards.

She has come possessed
Who admits the delusive light through the bouncing wall,
Possessed by the skies

She sleeps in the narrow trough yet she walks the dust
Yet raves at her will
On the madhouse boards worn thin by my walking tears.

And taken by light in her arms at long and dear last
I may without fail
Suffer the first vision that set fire to the stars.

141

ON THE MARRIAGE OF A VIRGIN

Waking alone in a multitude of loves when morning's light
Surprised in the opening of her nightlong eyes
His golden yesterday asleep upon the iris
And this day's sun leapt up the sky out of her thighs
Was miraculous virginity old as loaves and fishes,
Though the moment of a miracle is unending lightning
And the shipyards of Galilee's footprints hide a navy of doves.

No longer will the vibrations of the sun desire on
Her deepsea pillow where once she married alone,
Her heart all ears and eyes, lips catching the avalanche
Of the golden ghost who ringed with his streams her mercury bone,
Who under the lids of her windows hoisted his golden luggage,
For a man sleeps where fire leapt down and she learns through his
arm
That other sun, the jealous coursing of the unrivalled blood.

THE HUNCHBACK IN THE PARK

The hunchback in the park
A solitary mister
Propped between trees and water
From the opening of the garden lock
That lets the trees and water enter
Until the Sunday sombre bell at dark

Eating bread from a newspaper
Drinking water from the chained cup
That the children filled with gravel
In the fountain basin where I sailed my ship
Slept at night in a dog kennel
But nobody chained him up.

Like the park birds he came early
Like the water he sat down
And Mister they called Hey mister
The truant boys from the town
Running when he had heard them clearly
On out of sound

Past lake and rockery
Laughing when he shook his paper
Hunchbacked in mockery
Through the loud zoo of the willow groves
Dodging the park keeper
With his stick that picked up leaves.

And the old dog sleeper
Alone between nurses and swans
While the boys among willows

Made the tigers jump out of their eyes
To roar on the rockery stones
And the groves were blue with sailors

Made all day until bell time
A woman figure without fault
Straight as a young elm
Straight and tall from his crooked bones
That she might stand in the night
After the locks and chains

All night in the unmade park
After the railings and shrubberies
The birds the grass the trees the lake
And the wild boys innocent as strawberries
Had followed the hunchback
To his kennel in the dark.

143

AMONG THOSE KILLED IN THE DAWN RAID
WAS A MAN AGED A HUNDRED

When the morning was waking over the war
He put on his clothes and stepped out and he died,
The locks yawned loose and a blast blew them wide,
He dropped where he loved on the burst pavement stone
And the funeral grains of the slaughtered floor.
Tell his street on its back he stopped a sun
And the craters of his eyes grew springshoots and fire
When all the keys shot from the locks, and rang.
Dig no more for the chains of his grey-haired heart.
The heavenly ambulance drawn by a wound
Assembling waits for the spade's ring on the cage.

O keep his bones away from that common cart,
The morning is flying on the wings of his age
And a hundred storks perch on the sun's right hand.

CEREMONY AFTER A FIRE RAID

I

Myselves
The grievers
Grieve
Among the street burned to tireless death
A child of a few hours
With its kneading mouth
Charred on the black breast of the grave
The mother dug, and its arms full of fires.

Begin
With singing
Sing
Darkness kindled back into beginning
When the caught tongue nodded blind,
A star was broken
Into the centuries of the child
Myselves grieve now, and miracles cannot atone.

Forgive
Us forgive
Us
Your death that myselves the believers
May hold it in a great flood
Till the blood shall spurt,
And the dust shall sing like a bird
As the grains blow, as your death grows, through our heart.

Crying
Your dying
Cry,
Child beyond cockrow, by the fire-dwarfed
Street we chant the flying sea
In the body bereft.
Love is the last light spoken. Oh
Seed of sons in the loin of the black husk left.

II

I know not whether
Adam or Eve, the adorned holy bullock
Or the white ewe lamb
Or the chosen virgin
Laid in her snow
On the altar of London,
Was the first to die
In the cinder of the little skull,
O bride and bride groom
O Adam and Eve together
Lying in the lull
Under the sad breast of the head stone
White as the skeleton
Of the garden of Eden.

I know the legend
Of Adam and Eve is never for a second
Silent in my service
Over the dead infants
Over the one
Child who was priest and servants,
Word, singers, and tongue
In the cinder of the little skull,
Who was the serpent's
Night fall and the fruit like a sun,

Man and woman undone,
Beginning crumbled back to darkness
Bare as the nurseries
Of the garden of wilderness.

III

Into the organpipes and steeples
Of the luminous cathedrals,
Into the weathercocks' molten mouths
Rippling in twelve-winded circles,
Into the dead clock burning the hour
Over the urn of sabbaths
Over the whirling ditch of daybreak
Over the sun's hovel and the slum of fire
And the golden pavements laid in requiems,
Into the bread in a wheatfield of flames,
Into the wine burning like brandy,
The masses of the sea
The masses of the sea under
The masses of the infant-bearing sea
Erupt, fountain, and enter to utter for ever
Glory glory glory
The sundering ultimate kingdom of genesis' thunder.

145

LAST NIGHT I DIVED MY BEGGAR ARM

Last night I dived my beggar arm
Days deep in her breast that wore no heart
For me alone but only a rocked drum
Telling the heart I broke of a good habit

That her loving, unfriendly limbs
Would plunge my betrayal from sheet to sky

So the betrayed might learn in the sun beams
Of the death in a bed in another country.

146

POEM

Your breath was shed
Invisible to make
About the soiled undead
Night for my sake,

A raining trail
Intangible to them
With biter's tooth and tail
And cobweb drum,

A dark as deep
My love as a round wave
To hide the wolves of sleep
And mask the grave.

147

POEM IN OCTOBER

It was my thirtieth year to heaven
Woke to my hearing from harbour and neighbour wood
And the mussel pooled and the heron
Priested shore
The morning beckon

With water praying and call of seagull and rook
And the knock of sailing boats on the net webbed wall
    Myself to set foot
      That second
  In the still sleeping town and set forth.

  My birthday began with the water-
Birds and the birds of the winged trees flying my name
  Above the farms and the white horses
      And I rose
    In the rainy autumn
And walked abroad in a shower of all my days.
High tide and the heron dived when I took the road
    Over the border
      And the gates
  Of the town closed as the town awoke.

  A springful of larks in a rolling
Cloud and the roadside bushes brimming with whistling
  Blackbirds and the sun of October
      Summery
    On the hill's shoulder,
Here were fond climates and sweet singers suddenly
Come in the morning where I wandered and listened
    To the rain wringing
      Wind blow cold
  In the wood faraway under me.

  Pale rain over the dwindling harbour
And over the sea wet church the size of a snail
  With its horns through mist and the castle
      Brown as owls
    But all the gardens
Of spring and summer were blooming in the tall tales
Beyond the border and under the lark full cloud.

There could I marvel
    My birthday
Away but the weather turned around.

It turned away from the blithe country
And down the other air and the blue altered sky
   Streamed again a wonder of summer
        With apples
      Pears and red currants
And I saw in the turning so clearly a child's
Forgotten mornings when he walked with his mother
      Through the parables
        Of sun light
   And the legends of the green chapels

   And the twice told fields of infancy
That his tears burned my cheeks and his heart moved in mine.
   These were the woods the river and sea
        Where a boy
      In the listening
Summertime of the dead whispered the truth of his joy
To the trees and the stones and the fish in the tide.
      And the mystery
        Sang alive
   Still in the water and singingbirds.

   And there could·I marvel my birthday
Away but the weather turned around. And the true
   Joy of the long dead child sang burning
        In the sun.
      It was my thirtieth
Year to heaven stood there then in the summer noon
Though the town below lay leaved with October blood.
      O may my heart's truth
        Still be sung
   On this high hill in a year's turning.

NEW QUAY

Dear Tommy, please, from far, sciatic Kingsley
Borrow my eyes. The darkening sea flings Lea
And Perrins on the cockled tablecloth
Of mud and sand. And, like a sable moth,
A cloud against the glassy sun flutters his
Wings. It would be better if the shutters is
Shut. Sinister dark over Cardigan
Bay. No-good is abroad. I unhardy can
Hardly bear the din of No-good wracked dry on
The pebbles. It is time for the Black Lion
But there is only Buckley's unfrisky
Mild. Turned again, Worthington. Never whisky.
I sit at the open window, observing
The salty scene and my Playered gob curving
Down to the wild, umbrella'd, and french lettered
Beach, hearing rise slimy from the Welsh lechered
Caves the cries of the parchs and their flocks. I
Hear their laughter sly as gonococci.
There stinks a snoop in black. I'm thinking it
Is Mr. Jones the Cake, that winking-bit,
That hymning Gooseberry, that Bethel-worm
At whose ball-prying even death'll squirm
And button up. He minces among knickers,
That prince of pimps, that doyen of dung-lickers.
Over a rump on the clerical-grey seashore,
See how he stumbles. Hallelujah hee-haw!
His head's in a nest where no bird lays her egg.
He cuts himself on an elder's razor leg.
Sniff, here is sin! Now must he grapple, rise:
He snuggles deep among the chapel thighs,
And when the moist collection plate is passed
Puts in his penny, generous at last.

VISION AND PRAYER

i

Who
Are you
Who is born
In the next room
So loud to my own
That I can hear the womb
Opening and the dark run
Over the ghost and the dropped son
Behind the wall thin as a wren's bone?
In the birth bloody room unknown
To the burn and turn of time
And the heart print of man
Bows no baptism
But dark alone
Blessing on
The wild
Child.

I

Must lie
Still as stone
By the wren bone
Wall hearing the moan
Of the mother hidden
And the shadowed head of pain
Casting to-morrow like a thorn
And the midwives of miracle sing
Until the turbulent new born
Burns me his name and his flame
And the winged wall is torn
By his torrid crown
And the dark thrown
From his loin
To bright
Light.

When
The wren
Bone writhes down
And the first dawn
Furied by his stream
Swarms on the kingdom come
Of the dazzler of heaven
And the splashed mothering maiden
Who bore him with a bonfire in
His mouth and rocked him like a storm
I shall run lost in sudden
Terror and shining from
The once hooded room
Crying in vain
In the cauldron
Of his
Kiss

In
The spin
Of the sun
In the spuming
Cyclone of his wing
For I was lost who am
Crying at the man drenched throne
In the first fury of his stream
And the lightnings of adoration
Back to black silence melt and mourn
For I was lost who have come
To dumbfounding haven
And the finding one
And the high noon
Of his wound
Blinds my
Cry.

                    There
                  Crouched bare
                In the shrine
               Of   his   blazing
             Breast I shall waken
             To the judge blown bedlam
           Of the   uncaged sea bottom
       The cloud climb of the exhaling tomb
        And the bidden dust upsailing
         With his flame in every grain.
              O   spiral of   ascension
                From the vultured urn
                  Of the morning
                   Of man when
                    The land
                      And

                      The
                   Born sea
                 Praised the sun
                The finding one
              And upright Adam
             Sang upon origin!
           O the wings of the children!
       The woundward flight of the ancient
      Young from the canyons of oblivion!
       The sky stride of the always slain
           In   battle!   the   happening
              Of saints to their vision!
                The world winding home!
                And the whole pain
                   Flows   open
                    And   I
                     Die.

                    [182]

In the name of the lost who glory in
The swinish plains of carrion
Under the burial song
Of the birds of burden
Heavy with the drowned
And the green dust
And bearing
The ghost
From
The ground
Like pollen
On the black plume
And the beak of slime
I pray though I belong
Not wholly to that lamenting
Brethren for joy has moved within
The inmost marrow of my heart bone

That he who learns now the sun and moon
Of his mother's milk may return
Before the lips blaze and bloom
To the birth bloody room
Behind the wall's wren
Bone and be dumb
And the womb
That bore
For
All men
The adored
Infant light or
The dazzling prison
Yawn to his upcoming.
In the name of the wanton
Lost on the unchristened mountain
In the centre of dark I pray him

That he let the dead lie though they moan
For his briared hands to hoist them
To the shrine of his world's wound
And the blood drop's garden
Endure the stone
Blind host to sleep
In the dark
And deep
Rock
Awake
No heart bone
But let it break
On the mountain crown
Unbidden by the sun
And the beating dust be blown
Down to the river rooting plain
Under the night forever falling.

Forever falling night is a known
Star and country to the legion
Of sleepers whose tongue I toll
To mourn his deluging
Light through sea and soil
And we have come
To know all
Places
Ways
Mazes
Passages
Quarters and graves
Of the endless fall.
Now common lazarus
Of the charting sleepers prays
Never to awake and arise
For the country of death is the heart's size

[184]

And the star of the lost the shape of the eyes.
In the name of the fatherless
In the name of the unborn
And the undesirers
Of midwiving morning's
Hands or instruments
O in the name
Of no one
Now or
N o
One to
Be I pray
May the crimson
Sun spin a grave grey
And the colour of clay
Stream upon his martyrdom
In the interpreted evening
And the known dark of the earth amen.

I turn the corner of prayer and burn
In a blessing of the sudden
Sun. In the name of the damned
I would turn back and run
To the hidden land
But the loud sun
Christens down
The sky.
I
Am found.
O let him
Scald me and drown
Me in his world's wound.
His lightning answers my
Cry. My voice burns in his hand.
Now I am lost in the blinding
One. The sun roars at the prayer's end.

151

HOLY SPRING

O
Out of a bed of love
When that immortal hospital made one more move to soothe
The cureless counted body,
And ruin and his causes
Over the barbed and shooting sea assumed an army
And swept into our wounds and houses,
I climb to greet the war in which I have no heart but only
That one dark I owe my light,
Call for confessor and wiser mirror but there is none
To glow after the god stoning night
And I am struck as lonely as a holy maker by the sun.

No
Praise that the spring time is all
Gabriel and radiant shrubbery as the morning grows joyful
Out of the woebegone pyre
And the multitude's sultry tear turns cool on the weeping wall,
My arising prodigal
Sun the father his quiver full of the infants of pure fire,
But blessed be hail and upheaval
That uncalm still it is sure alone to stand and sing
Alone in the husk of man's home
And the mother and toppling house of the holy spring,
If only for a last time.

151

A WINTER'S TALE

It is a winter's tale
That the snow blind twilight ferries over the lakes
And floating fields from the farm in the cup of the vales,
Gliding windless through the hand folded flakes,
The pale breath of cattle at the stealthy sail,

And the stars falling cold,
And the smell of hay in the snow, and the far owl
Warning among the folds, and the frozen hold
Flocked with the sheep white smoke of the farm house cowl
In the river wended vales where the tale was told.

Once when the world turned old
On a star of faith pure as the drifting bread,
As the food and flames of the snow, a man unrolled
The scrolls of fire that burned in his heart and head,
Torn and alone in a farm house in a fold

Of fields. And burning then
In his firelit island ringed by the winged snow
And the dung hills white as wool and the hen
Roosts sleeping chill till the flame of the cock crow
Combs through the mantled yards and the morning men

Stumble out with their spades,
The cattle stirring, the mousing cat stepping shy,
The puffed birds hopping and hunting, the milkmaids
Gentle in their clogs over the fallen sky,
And all the woken farm at its white trades,

[187]

He knelt, he wept, he prayed,
By the spit and the black pot in the log bright light
And the cup and the cut bread in the dancing shade,
In the muffled house, in the quick of night,
At the point of love, forsaken and afraid.

He knelt on the cold stones,
He wept from the crest of grief, he prayed to the veiled sky
May his hunger go howling on bare white bones
Past the statues of the stables and the sky roofed sties
And the duck pond glass and the blinding byres alone

Into the home of prayers
And fires where he should prowl down the cloud
Of his snow blind love and rush in the white lairs.
His naked need struck him howling and bowed
Though no sound flowed down the hand folded air

But only the wind strung
Hunger of birds in the fields of the bread of water, tossed
In high corn and the harvest melting on their tongues.
And his nameless need bound him burning and lost
When cold as snow he should run the wended vales among

The rivers mouthed in night,
And drown in the drifts of his need, and lie curled caught
In the always desiring centre of the white
Inhuman cradle and the bride bed forever sought
By the believer lost and the hurled outcast of light.

Deliver him, he cried,
By losing him all in love, and cast his need
Alone and naked in the engulfing bride,
Never to flourish in the fields of the white seed
Or flower under the time dying flesh astride.

Listen. The minstrels sing
In the departed villages. The nightingale,
Dust in the buried wood, flies on the grains of her wings
And spells on the winds of the dead his winter's tale.
The voice of the dust of water from the withered spring

Is telling. The wizened
Stream with bells and baying water bounds. The dew rings
On the gristed leaves and the long gone glistening
Parish of snow. The carved mouths in the rock are wind swept
    strings.
Time sings through the intricately dead snow drop. Listen.

It was a hand or sound
In the long ago land that glided the dark door wide
And there outside on the bread of the ground
A she bird rose and rayed like a burning bride.
A she bird dawned, and her breast with snow and scarlet downed.

Look. And the dancers move
On the departed, snow bushed green, wanton in moon light
As a dust of pigeons. Exulting, the graved hooved
Horses, centaur dead, turn and tread the drenched white
Paddocks in the farms of birds. The dead oak walks for love.

The carved limbs in the rock
Leap, as to trumpets. Calligraphy of the old
Leaves is dancing. Lines of age on the stones weave in a flock.
And the harp shaped voice of the water's dust plucks in a fold
Of fields. For love, the long ago she bird rises. Look.

And the wild wings were raised
Above her folded head, and the soft feathered voice
Was flying through the house as though the she bird praised
And all the elements of the slow fall rejoiced
That a man knelt alone in the cup of the vales,

In the mantle and calm,
By the spit and the black pot in the log bright light.
And the sky of birds in the plumed voice charmed
Him up and he ran like a wind after the kindling flight
Past the blind barns and byres of the windless farm.

In the poles of the year
When black birds died like priests in the cloaked hedge row
And over the cloth of counties the far hills rode near,
Under the one leaved trees ran a scarecrow of snow
And fast through the drifts of the thickets antlered like deer,

Rags and prayers down the knee-
Deep hillocks and loud on the numbed lakes,
All night lost and long wading in the wake of the she-
Bird through the times and lands and tribes of the slow flakes.
Listen and look where she sails the goose plucked sea,

The sky, the bird, the bride,
The cloud, the need, the planted stars, the joy beyond
The fields of seed and the time dying flesh astride,
The heavens, the heaven, the grave, the burning font.
In the far ago land the door of his death glided wide

And the bird descended.
On a bread white hill over the cupped farm
And the lakes and floating fields and the river wended
Vales where he prayed to come to the last harm
And the home of prayers and fires, the tale ended.

The dancing perishes
On the white, no longer growing green, and, minstrel dead,
The singing breaks in the snow shoed villages of wishes
That once cut the figures of birds on the deep bread
And over the glazed lakes skated the shapes of fishes

Flying. The rite is shorn
Of nightingale and centaur dead horse. The springs wither
Back. Lines of age sleep on the stones till trumpeting dawn.
Exultation lies down. Time buries the spring weather
That belled and bounded with the fossil and the dew reborn.

For the bird lay bedded
In a choir of wings, as though she slept or died,
And the wings glided wide and he was hymned and wedded,
And through the thighs of the engulfing bride,
The woman breasted and the heaven headed

Bird, he was brought low,
Burning in the bride bed of love, in the whirl-
Pool at the wanting centre, in the folds
Of paradise, in the spun bud of the world.
And she rose with him flowering in her melting snow.

152

A REFUSAL TO MOURN THE DEATH, BY FIRE, OF A CHILD IN LONDON

Never until the mankind making
Bird beast and flower
Fathering and all humbling darkness
Tells with silence the last light breaking
And the still hour
Is come of the sea tumbling in harness

And I must enter again the round
Zion of the water bead
And the synagogue of the ear of corn
Shall I let pray the shadow of a sound
Or sow my salt seed
In the least valley of sackcloth to mourn

The majesty and burning of the child's death.
I shall not murder
The mankind of her going with a grave truth
Nor blaspheme down the stations of the breath
With any further
Elegy of innocence and youth.

Deep with the first dead lies London's daughter,
Robed in the long friends,
The grains beyond age, the dark veins of her mother,
Secret by the unmourning water
Of the riding Thames.
After the first death, there is no other.

153

THIS SIDE OF THE TRUTH
(for Llewelyn)

This side of the truth,
You may not see, my son,
King of your blue eyes
In the blinding country of youth,
That all is undone,
Under the unminding skies,
Of innocence and guilt
Before you move to make
One gesture of the heart or head,
Is gathered and spilt
Into the winding dark
Like the dust of the dead.

Good and bad, two ways
Of moving about your death
By the grinding sea,

King of your heart in the blind days,
Blow away like breath,
Go crying through you and me
And the souls of all men
Into the innocent
Dark, and the guilty dark, and good
Death, and bad death, and then
In the last element
Fly like the stars' blood,

Like the sun's tears,
Like the moon's seed, rubbish
And fire, the flying rant
Of the sky, king of your six years.
And the wicked wish,
Down the beginning of plants
And animals and birds,
Water and light, the earth and sky,
Is cast before you move,
And all your deeds and words,
Each truth, each lie,
Die in unjudging love.

154

THE CONVERSATION OF PRAYER

The conversation of prayers about to be said
By the child going to bed and the man on the stairs
Who climbs to his dying love in her high room,
The one not caring to whom in his sleep he will move
And the other full of tears that she will be dead,

Turns in the dark on the sound they know will arise
Into the answering skies from the green ground,

From the man on the stairs and the child by his bed.
The sound about to be said in the two prayers
For the sleep in a safe land and the love who dies

Will be the same grief flying. Whom shall they calm?
Shall the child sleep unharmed or the man be crying?
The conversation of prayers about to be said
Turns on the quick and the dead, and the man on the stairs
To-night shall find no dying but alive and warm

In the fire of his care his love in the high room.
And the child not caring to whom he climbs his prayer
Shall drown in a grief as deep as his true grave,
And mark the dark eyed wave, through the eyes of sleep,
Dragging him up the stairs to one who lies dead.

155

LIE STILL, SLEEP BECALMED

Lie still, sleep becalmed, sufferer with the wound
In the throat, burning and turning. All night afloat
On the silent sea we have heard the sound
That came from the wound wrapped in the salt sheet.

Under the mile off moon we trembled listening
To the sea sound flowing like blood from the loud wound
And when the salt sheet broke in a storm of singing
The voices of all the drowned swam on the wind.

Open a pathway through the slow sad sail,
Throw wide to the wind the gates of the wandering boat
For my voyage to begin to the end of my wound,
We heard the sea sound sing, we saw the salt sheet tell.
Lie still, sleep becalmed, hide the mouth in the throat,
Or we shall obey, and ride with you through the drowned.

FERN HILL

Now as I was young and easy under the apple boughs
About the lilting house and happy as the grass was green,
   The night above the dingle starry,
    Time let me hail and climb
   Golden in the heydays of his eyes,
And honoured among wagons I was prince of the apple towns
And once below a time I lordly had the trees and leaves
    Trail with daisies and barley
   Down the rivers of the windfall light.

And as I was green and carefree, famous among the barns
About the happy yard and singing as the farm was home,
   In the sun that is young once only,
    Time let me play and be
   Golden in the mercy of his means,
And green and golden I was huntsman and herdsman, the calves
Sang to my horn, the foxes on the hills barked clear and cold,
    And the sabbath rang slowly
   In the pebbles of the holy streams.

All the sun long it was running, it was lovely, the hay
Fields high as the house, the tunes from the chimneys, it was air
   And playing, lovely and watery
    And fire green as grass.
   And nightly under the simple stars
As I rode to sleep the owls were bearing the farm away,
All the moon long I heard, blessed among stables, the nightjars
   Flying with the ricks, and the horses
    Flashing into the dark.

And then to awake, and the farm, like a wanderer white
With the dew, come back, the cock on his shoulder: it was all

Shining, it was Adam and maiden,
  The sky gathered again
And the sun grew round that very day.
So it must have been after the birth of the simple light
In the first, spinning place, the spellbound horses walking warm
  Out of the whinnying green stable
    On to the fields of praise.

And honoured among foxes and pheasants by the gay house
Under the new made clouds and happy as the heart was long,
  In the sun born over and over,
    I ran my heedless ways,
  My wishes raced through the house high hay
And nothing I cared, at my sky blue trades, that time allows
In all his tuneful turning so few and such morning songs
  Before the children green and golden
    Follow him out of grace,

Nothing I cared, in the lamb white days, that time would take me
Up to the swallow thronged loft by the shadow of my hand,
  In the moon that is always rising,
    Nor that riding to sleep
  I should hear him fly with the high fields
And wake to the farm forever fled from the childless land.
Oh as I was young and easy in the mercy of his means,
    Time held me green and dying
  Though I sang in my chains like the sea.

157

IN MY CRAFT OR SULLEN ART

In my craft or sullen art
Exercised in the still night
When only the moon rages

[196]

And the lovers lie abed
With all their griefs in their arms,
I labour by singing light
Not for ambition or bread
Or the strut and trade of charms
On the ivory stages
But for the common wages
Of their most secret heart.

Not for the proud man apart
From the raging moon I write
On these spindrift pages
Nor for the towering dead
With their nightingales and psalms
But for the lovers, their arms
Round the griefs of the ages,
Who pay no praise or wages
Nor heed my craft or art.

158

IN COUNTRY SLEEP

I

Never and never, my girl riding far and near
In the land of the hearthstone tales, and spelled asleep,
Fear or believe that the wolf in a sheepwhite hood
Loping and bleating roughly and blithely shall leap,
My dear, my dear,
Out of a lair in the flocked leaves in the dew dipped year
To eat your heart in the house in the rosy wood.

Sleep, good, for ever, slow and deep, spelled rare and wise,
My girl ranging the night in the rose and shire
Of the hobnail tales: no gooseherd or swine will turn

Into a homestall king or hamlet of fire
                                        And prince of ice
To court the honeyed heart from your side before sunrise
In a spinney of ringed boys and ganders, spike and burn,

Nor the innocent lie in the rooting dingle wooed
And staved, and riven among plumes my rider weep.
From the broomed witch's spume you are shielded by fern
And flower of country sleep and the greenwood keep.
                                        Lie fast and soothed,
Safe be and smooth from the bellows of the rushy brood.
Never, my girl, until tolled to sleep by the stern

Bell believe or fear that the rustic shade or spell
Shall harrow and snow the blood while you ride wide and near,
For who unmanningly haunts the mountain ravened eaves
Or skulks in the dell moon but moonshine echoing clear
                                        From the starred well?
A hill touches an angel. Out of a saint's cell
The nightbird lauds through nunneries and domes of leaves

Her robin breasted tree, three Marys in the rays.
Sanctum sanctorum the animal eye of the wood
In the rain telling its beads, and the gravest ghost
The owl at its knelling. Fox and holt kneel before blood.
                                        Now the tales praise
The star rise at pasture and nightlong the fables graze
On the lord's-table of the bowing grass. Fear most

For ever of all not the wolf in his baaing hood
Nor the tusked prince, in the ruttish farm, at the rind
And mire of love, but the Thief as meek as the dew.
The country is holy: O bide in that country kind,
                                        Know the green good,
Under the prayer wheeling moon in the rosy wood
Be shielded by chant and flower and gay may you

Lie in grace. Sleep spelled at rest in the lowly house
In the squirrel nimble grove, under linen and thatch
And star: held and blessed, though you scour the high four
Winds, from the dousing shade and the roarer at the latch,
                                        Cool in your vows.
Yet out of the beaked, web dark and the pouncing boughs
Be you sure the Thief will seek a way sly and sure

And sly as snow and meek as dew blown to the thorn,
This night and each vast night until the stern bell talks
In the tower and tolls to sleep over the stalls
Of the hearthstone tales my own, lost love; and the soul walks
                                        The waters shorn.
This night and each night since the falling star you were born,
Ever and ever he finds a way, as the snow falls,

As the rain falls, hail on the fleece, as the vale mist rides
Through the haygold stalls, as the dew falls on the wind-
Milled dust of the apple tree and the pounded islands
Of the morning leaves, as the star falls, as the winged
                                        Apple seed glides,
And falls, and flowers in the yawning wound at our sides,
As the world falls, silent as the cyclone of silence.

II

Night and the reindeer on the clouds above the haycocks
And the wings of the great roc ribboned for the fair!
The leaping saga of prayer! And high, there, on the hare-
                                        Heeled winds the rooks
Cawing from their black bethels soaring, the holy books
Of birds! Among the cocks like fire the red fox

Burning! Night and the vein of birds in the winged, sloe wrist
Of the wood! Pastoral beat of blood through the laced leaves!

The stream from the priest black wristed spinney and sleeves
                                    Of thistling frost
Of the nightingale's din and tale! The upgiven ghost
Of the dingle torn to singing and the surpliced

Hill of cypresses! The din and tale in the skimmed
Yard of the buttermilk rain on the pail! The sermon
Of blood! The bird loud vein! The saga from mermen
                                    To seraphim
Leaping! The gospel rooks! All tell, this night, of him
Who comes as red as the fox and sly as the heeled wind.

Illumination of music! The lulled black-backed
Gull, on the wave with sand in its eyes! And the foal moves
Through the shaken greensward lake, silent, on moonshod hooves,
                                    In the winds' wakes.
Music of elements, that a miracle makes!
Earth, air, water, fire, singing into the white act,

The haygold haired, my love asleep, and the rift blue
Eyed, in the haloed house, in her rareness and hilly
High riding, held and blessed and true, and so stilly
                                    Lying the sky
Might cross its planets, the bell weep, night gather her eyes,
The Thief fall on the dead like the willy nilly dew,

Only for the turning of the earth in her holy
Heart! Slyly, slowly, hearing the wound in her side go
Round the sun, he comes to my love like the designed snow,
                                    And truly he
Flows to the strand of flowers like the dew's ruly sea,
And surely he sails like the ship shape clouds. Oh he

Comes designed to my love to steal not her tide raking

[200]

Wound, nor her riding high, nor her eyes, nor kindled hair,
But her faith that each vast night and the saga of prayer
                                        He comes to take
Her faith that this last night for his unsacred sake
He comes to leave her in the lawless sun awaking

Naked and forsaken to grieve he will not come.
Ever and ever by all your vows believe and fear
My dear this night he comes and night without end my dear
                                        Since you were born:
And you shall wake, from country sleep, this dawn and each first
    dawn,
Your faith as deathless as the outcry of the ruled sun.

159

OVER SIR JOHN'S HILL

Over Sir John's hill,
The hawk on fire hangs still;
In a hoisted cloud, at drop of dusk, he pulls to his claws
And gallows, up the rays of his eyes the small birds of the bay
And the shrill child's play
Wars
Of the sparrows and such who swansing, dusk, in wrangling
    hedges.
And blithely they squawk
To fiery tyburn over the wrestle of elms until
The flashed the noosed hawk
Crashes, and slowly the fishing holy stalking heron
In the river Towy below bows his tilted headstone.

Flash, and the plumes crack,
And a black cap of jack-
Daws Sir John's just hill dons, and again the gulled birds hare

To the hawk on fire, the halter height, over Towy's fins,
In a whack of wind.
There
Where the elegiac fisherbird stabs and paddles
In the pebbly dab-filled
Shallow and sedge, and 'dilly dilly', calls the loft hawk,
'Come and be killed,'
I open the leaves of the water at a passage
Of psalms and shadows among the pincered sandcrabs prancing

And read, in a shell,
Death clear as a buoy's bell:
All praise of the hawk on fire in hawk-eyed dusk be sung,
When his viperish fuse hangs looped with flames under the brand
Wing, and blest shall
Young
Green chickens of the bay and bushes cluck, 'dilly dilly,
Come let us die.'
We grieve as the blithe birds, never again, leave shingle and elm,
The heron and I,
I young Aesop fabling to the near night by the dingle
Of eels, saint heron hymning in the shell-hung distant

Crystal harbour vale
Where the sea cobbles sail,
And wharves of water where the walls dance and the white cranes
    stilt.
It is the heron and I, under judging Sir John's elmed
Hill, tell-tale the knelled
Guilt
Of the led-astray birds whom God, for their breast of whistles,
Have mercy on,
God in his whirlwind silence save, who marks the sparrows hail,
For their souls' song.
Now the heron grieves in the weeded verge. Through windows
Of dusk and water I see the tilting whispering

Heron, mirrored, go,
As the snapt feathers snow,
Fishing in the tear of the Towy. Only a hoot owl
Hollows, a grassblade blown in cupped hands, in the looted elms
And no green cocks or hens
Shout
Now on Sir John's hill. The heron, ankling the scaly
Lowlands of the waves
Makes all the music; and I who hear the tune of the slow,
Wear-willow river, grave,
Before the lunge of the night, the notes on this time-shaken
Stone for the sake of the souls of the slain birds sailing.

160

IN THE WHITE GIANT'S THIGH

Through throats where many rivers meet, the curlews cry,
Under the conceiving moon, on the high chalk hill,
And there this night I walk in the white giant's thigh
Where barren as boulders women lie longing still

To labour and love though they lay down long ago.

Through throats where many rivers meet, the women pray,
Pleading in the waded bay for the seed to flow
Though the names on their weed grown stones are rained away,

And alone in the night's eternal, curving act
They yearn with tongues of curlews for the unconceived
And immemorial sons of the cudgelling, hacked

Hill. Who once in gooseskin winter loved all ice leaved
In the courters' lanes, or twined in the ox roasting sun

[203]

In the wains tonned so high that the wisps of the hay
Clung to the pitching clouds, or gay with any one
Young as they in the after milking moonlight lay

Under the lighted shapes of faith and their moonshade
Petticoats galed high, or shy with the rough riding boys,
Now clasp me to their grains in the gigantic glade,

Who once, green countries since, were a hedgerow of joys.
Time by, their dust was flesh the swineherd rooted sly,
Flared in the reek of the wiving sty with the rush
Light of his thighs, spreadeagle to the dunghill sky,
Or with their orchard man in the core of the sun's bush
Rough as cows' tongues and thrashed with brambles their butter-
    milk
Manes, under his quenchless summer barbed gold to the bone,

Or rippling soft in the spinney moon as the silk
And ducked and draked white lake that harps to a hail stone.

Who once were a bloom of wayside brides in the hawed house
And heard the lewd, wooed field flow to the coming frost,
The scurrying, furred small friars squeal, in the dowse
Of day, in the thistle aisles, till the white owl crossed

Their breast, the vaulting does roister, the horned bucks climb
Quick in the wood at love, where a torch of foxes foams,
All birds and beasts of the linked night uproar and chime

And the mole snout blunt under his pilgrimage of domes,
Or, butter fat goosegirls, bounced in a gambo bed,

[204]

Their breasts full of honey, under their gander king
Trounced by his wings in the hissing shippen, long dead
And gone that barley dark where their clogs danced in the spring,
And their firefly hairpins flew, and the ricks ran round—

(But nothing bore, no mouthing babe to the veined hives
Hugged, and barren and bare on Mother Goose's ground
They with the simple Jacks were a boulder of wives)—

Now curlew cry me down to kiss the mouths of their dust.

The dust of their kettles and clocks swings to and fro
Where the hay rides now or the bracken kitchens rust
As the arc of the billhooks that flashed the hedges low
And cut the birds' boughs that the minstrel sap ran red.
They from houses where the harvest kneels, hold me hard,
Who heard the tall bell sail down the Sundays of the dead
And the rain wring out its tongues on the faded yard,
Teach me the love that is evergreen after the fall leaved
Grave, after Belovéd on the grass gulfed cross is scrubbed
Off by the sun and Daughters no longer grieved
Save by their long desirers in the fox cubbed
Streets or hungering in the crumbled wood: to these
Hale dead and deathless do the women of the hill
Love for ever meridian through the courters' trees

And the daughters of darkness flame like Fawkes fires still.

LAMENT

When I was a windy boy and a bit
And the black spit of the chapel fold,

(Sighed the old ram rod, dying of women),
I tiptoed shy in the gooseberry wood,
The rude owl cried like a telltale tit,
I skipped in a blush as the big girls rolled
Ninepin down on the donkeys' common,
And on seesaw sunday nights I wooed
Whoever I would with my wicked eyes,
The whole of the moon I could love and leave
All the green leaved little weddings' wives
In the coal black bush and let them grieve.

When I was a gusty man and a half
And the black beast of the beetles' pews,
(Sighed the old ram rod, dying of bitches),
Not a boy and a bit in the wick-
Dipping moon and drunk as a new dropped calf,
I whistled all night in the twisted flues,
Midwives grew in the midnight ditches,
And the sizzling beds of the town cried, Quick!—
Whenever I dove in a breast high shoal,
Wherever I ramped in the clover quilts,
Whatsoever I did in the coal-
Black night, I left my quivering prints.

When I was a man you could call a man
And the black cross of the holy house,
(Sighed the old ram rod, dying of welcome),
Brandy and ripe in my bright, bass prime,
No springtailed tom in the red hot town
With every simmering woman his mouse
But a hillocky bull in the swelter
Of summer come in his great good time
To the sultry, biding herds, I said,
Oh, time enough when the blood creeps cold,
And I lie down but to sleep in bed,
For my sulking, skulking, coal black soul!

When I was a half of the man I was
And serve me right as the preachers warn,
(Sighed the old ram rod, dying of downfall),
No flailing calf or cat in a flame
Or hickory bull in milky grass
But a black sheep with a crumpled horn,
At last the soul from its foul mousehole
Slunk pouting out when the limp time came;
And I gave my soul a blind, slashed eye,
Gristle and rind, and a roarers' life,
And I shoved it into the coal black sky
To find a woman's soul for a wife.

Now I am a man no more no more
And a black reward for a roaring life,
(Sighed the old ram rod, dying of strangers),
Tidy and cursed in my dove cooed room
I lie down thin and hear the good bells jaw—
For, oh, my soul found a sunday wife
In the coal black sky and she bore angels!
Harpies around me out of her womb!
Chastity prays for me, piety sings,
Innocence sweetens my last black breath,
Modesty hides my thighs in her wings,
And all the deadly virtues plague my death!

162

DO NOT GO GENTLE INTO THAT GOOD NIGHT

Do not go gentle into that good night,
Old age should burn and rave at close of day;
Rage, rage against the dying of the light.

Though wise men at their end know dark is right,
Because their words had forked no lightning they
Do not go gentle into that good night.

Good men, the last wave by, crying how bright
Their frail deeds might have danced in a green bay,
Rage, rage against the dying of the light.

Wild men who caught and sang the sun in flight,
And learn, too late, they grieved it on its way,
Do not go gentle into that good night.

Grave men, near death, who see with blinding sight
Blind eyes could blaze like meteors and be gay,
Rage, rage against the dying of the light.

And you, my father, there on the sad height,
Curse, bless, me now with your fierce tears, I pray.
Do not go gentle into that good night.
Rage, rage against the dying of the light.

163

POEM ON HIS BIRTHDAY

In the mustardseed sun,
By full tilt river and switchback sea
    Where the cormorants scud,
In his house on stilts high among beaks
    And palavers of birds
This sandgrain day in the bent bay's grave
    He celebrates and spurns
His driftwood thirty-fifth wind turned age;
    Herons spire and spear.

Under and round him go
Flounders, gulls, on their cold, dying trails,
   Doing what they are told,
Curlews aloud in the congered waves
   Work at their ways to death,
And the rhymer in the long tongued room,
   Who tolls his birthday bell,
Toils towards the ambush of his wounds;
   Herons, steeple stemmed, bless.

   In the thistledown fall,
He sings towards anguish; finches fly
   In the claw tracks of hawks
On a seizing sky; small fishes glide
   Through wynds and shells of drowned
Ship towns to pastures of otters. He
   In his slant, racking house
And the hewn coils of his trade perceives
   Herons walk in their shroud,

   The livelong river's robe
Of minnows wreathing around their prayer;
   And far at sea he knows,
Who slaves to his crouched, eternal end
   Under a serpent cloud,
Dolphins dive in their turnturtle dust,
   The rippled seals streak down
To kill and their own tide daubing blood
   Slides good in the sleek mouth.

   In a cavernous, swung
Wave's silence, wept white angelus knells.
   Thirty-five bells sing struck
On skull and scar where his loves lie wrecked,
   Steered by the falling stars.
And to-morrow weeps in a blind cage

Terror will rage apart
Before chains break to a hammer flame
And love unbolts the dark

And freely he goes lost
In the unknown, famous light of great
And fabulous, dear God.
Dark is a way and light is a place,
Heaven that never was
Nor will be ever is always true,
And, in that brambled void,
Plenty as blackberries in the woods
The dead grow for His joy.

There he might wander bare
With the spirits of the horseshoe bay
Or the stars' seashore dead,
Marrow of eagles, the roots of whales
And wishbones of wild geese,
With blessed, unborn God and His Ghost,
And every soul His priest,
Gulled and chanter in young Heaven's fold
Be at cloud quaking peace,

But dark is a long way.
He, on the earth of the night, alone
With all the living, prays,
Who knows the rocketing wind will blow
The bones out of the hills,
And the scythed boulders bleed, and the last
Rage shattered waters kick
Masts and fishes to the still quick stars,
Faithlessly unto Him

Who is the light of old
And air shaped Heaven where souls grow wild
As horses in the foam:

Oh, let me midlife mourn by the shrined
    And druid herons' vows
The voyage to ruin I must run,
    Dawn ships clouted aground,
Yet, though I cry with tumbledown tongue,
    Count my blessings aloud:

    Four elements and five
Senses, and man a spirit in love
    Tangling through this spun slime
To his nimbus bell cool kingdom come
    And the lost, moonshine domes,
And the sea that hides his secret selves
    Deep in its black, base bones,
Lulling of spheres in the seashell flesh,
    And this last blessing most,

    That the closer I move
To death, one man through his sundered hulks,
    The louder the sun blooms
And the tusked, ramshackling sea exults;
    And every wave of the way
And gale I tackle, the whole world then,
    With more triumphant faith
That ever was since the world was said,
    Spins its morning of praise,

    I hear the bouncing hills
Grow larked and greener at berry brown
    Fall and the dew larks sing
Taller this thunderclap spring, and how
    More spanned with angels ride
The mansouled fiery islands! Oh,
    Holier then their eyes,
And my shining men no more alone
    As I sail out to die.

UNFINISHED POEMS

IN COUNTRY HEAVEN

Always when he, in country heaven,
>   (Whom my heart hears),
Crosses the breast of the praising East, and kneels,
>   Humble in all his planets,
>   And weeps on the abasing hill,

Then in the delight and grove of beasts and birds
>   And the canonized valley
>   Where the dewfall stars sing grazing still
>   And the angels whirr like pheasants
>   Through naves of leaves,

>   Light and his tears glide down together
>   (O hand in hand)
From the country eyes, salt and sun, star and woe
>   Down the cheek bones and whinnying
>   Downs into the low browsing dark.

Housed in hamlets of heaven swing the loft lamps,
>   In the black buried spinneys
>   Bushes and owls blow out like candles,
>   And seraphic fields of shepherds
>   Fade with their rose-

>   White, God's bright, flocks, the belled lambs leaping,
>   (His gentle kind);
The shooting star hawk statued blind in a cloud
>   Over the blackamoor shires
>   Hears the belfries and the cobbles

[215]

Of the twelve apostles' towns ring in his night;
    And the long fox like fire
  Prowls flaming among the cockerels
    In the farms of heaven's keeping,
                        But they sleep sound.

  For the fifth element is pity,
                        (Pity for death). . . .

(b)

ELEGY

Too proud to die, broken and blind he died
The darkest way, and did not turn away,
A cold kind man brave in his narrow pride

On that darkest day. Oh, forever may
He lie lightly, at last, on the last, crossed
Hill, under the grass, in love, and there grow

Young among the long flocks, and never lie lost
Or still all the numberless days of his death, though
Above all he longed for his mother's breast

Which was rest and dust, and in the kind ground
The darkest justice of death, blind and unblessed.
Let him find no rest but be fathered and found,

I prayed in the crouching room, by his blind bed,
In the muted house, one minute before
Noon, and night, and light. The rivers of the dead

Veined his poor hand I held, and I saw
Through his unseeing eyes to the roots of the sea.
[An old tormented man three-quarters blind,

I am not too proud to cry that He and he
Will never never go out of my mind.
All his bones crying, and poor in all but pain,

Being innocent, he dreaded that he died
Hating his God, but what he was was plain:
An old kind man brave in his burning pride.

The sticks of the house were his; his books he owned.
Even as a baby he had never cried;
Nor did he now, save to his secret wound.

Out of his eyes I saw the last light glide.
Here among the light of the lording sky
An old blind man is with me where I go

Walking in the meadows of his son's eye
On whom a world of ills came down like snow.
He cried as he died, fearing at last the spheres'

Last sound, the world going out without a breath:
Too proud to cry, too frail to check the tears,
And caught between two nights, blindness and death.

O deepest wound of all that he should die
On that darkest day. Oh, he could hide
The tears out of his eyes, too proud to cry.

Until I die he will not leave my side.]

APPENDIX II
EARLY POEMS
(Written before the poet's sixteenth birthday)

THE SONG OF THE MISCHIEVOUS DOG

There are many who say that a dog has its day,
    And a cat has a number of lives;
There are others who think that a lobster is pink,
    And that bees never work in their hives.
There are fewer, of course, who insist that a horse
    Has a horn and two humps on its head,
And a fellow who jests that a mare can build nests
    Is as rare as a donkey that's red.
Yet in spite of all this, I have moments of bliss,
    For I cherish a passion for bones,
And though doubtful of biscuit, I'm willing to risk it,
    And I love to chase rabbits and stones.
But my greatest delight is to take a good bite
    At a calf that is plump and delicious;
And if I indulge in a bite at a bulge,
    Let's hope you won't think me too vicious.

FOREST PICTURE

Calm and strange is this evening hour in the forest,
Carven domes of green are the trees by the pathway,
Infinite shadowy isles lie silent before me,
Summer is heavy with age, and leans upon Autumn.

All the land is ripe. There is no motion
Down the long bays of blue that those cloudy headlands
Sleep above in the glow of a fading sunset;
All things rest in the will of purpose triumphant.

Outlines melting into a vague immensity
Fade, the green gloom grows darker, and deeper the dusk:
Hark! a voice and laughter—the living and loving
Down these fantastic avenues pass like shadows.

(iii)

MISSING

Seek him, thou sun, in the dread wilderness,
For that he loved thee, seek thou him and bless
His upturned face with one divine caress.

Lightly, thou wind, over his dear, dark head,
Where now the wings of dreamless sleep are spread,
Whisper a benediction for the dead.

Softly, thou rain—and for his mother's sake,
Shed thou thy tears on him; he will not wake,
No weeping through that deep repose can break.

(iv)

IN DREAMS

And in her garden grow the fleur de lys,
    The tall mauve iris of a sleeping clime.
Their pale, ethereal beauty seems to be
    The frail and delicate breath of even-time.

And night, who stooped to kiss the pallid leaves
   To that strange colour, sighing gently, grieves
For her who walks within her garden-close.
   Somehow it seems, amid the evening haze,
That in her garden, rather than the days,
   There should be night for ever, and no rose,
But only iris on their slender stalks
Along the borders of the garden-walks.

     .   .   .   .   .

Her garden blooms with iris, and it seems
The moons are white flames, like the moons in dreams.

(v)

IDYLL OF UNFORGETFULNESS

To have seen countries which were glorious,
Immutable, and ardourously consecrated;
To have known them in their blue-hued valiance,
Felt their serenity of ripple-woven loveliness;
To have heard their vague, rhapsodic singings,
Their silences in silver quietness of sleep,
And listened when a slow, starred slumber wrapt the moon,
To the voices of the wind caught in the cradle-petals of the night:
These were my desires, eternal as mountains,
These were the whisperings that sighed on my lips at dusk,
These the imaginings, tender and blossomed with futility,
That played in voiceless frolic at the threshold of my heart.
These countries I have not visioned,
Which bathe themselves in a ravishment of snow;
Their grasses, each a tiny ecstasy,
Have not adored my body as it softly smoothed their skin.
But I have known the still ardour of equability;
I have known the mystery of the sea to be mantled about me;

I have felt the silk wind brush my lips;
I have made my throat an arbour for forgotten songs.
The sea has been breeze-serene sapphire,
And blue-tipped birds have rippled it,
And the sun has smoothed it with quiet fire,
And I have reflected its colours in the peace of my eyes;
It has been vague, and made of shadow,
With little, odd mists waved in the path of its echo,
When everything slept and the smell of the waves was strange;
The foam has lingered into white, little flowers,
And changed with the wind into indistinct patterns of frolic,
And my fingers have touched the glass of the waters,
And hours made little I have dipped my arms in their rapture;
Little white-lipped faces have peered up at me,
And eyes have been grove-green catching mine from the depth of
  the silence;
Voices have called, and the answers lemural whispers from the sea;
And covering all has been a quietude, and a singing from flake-
  bare throats.
Now the sea has a flowering of foam;
Hidden in delicate drifts of mist are they that beckon,
They of the pale, sea-wan beauty, they of the home
Of the pale-green, delicate fishes, silver as sighs;
Their voices are dim; they have passed,
In the carpeting of the dusk, obscurely and elusively,
Enveloping themselves in the laden eve;
The darkness is illimitable, green shadow,
And the whisper caught in its pageant of tawny pearl,
Green-shadowed panoply enveloping all its strangeness and
  softness of stealth.

(vi)

OF ANY FLOWER

Hourly I sigh,
For all things are leaf-like
And cloud-like.

Flowerly I die,
For all things are grief-like
And shroud-like.

(vii)

CLOWN IN THE MOON

My tears are like the quiet drift
Of petals from some magic rose;
And all my grief flows from the rift
Of unremembered skies and snows.

I think, that if I touched the earth,
It would crumble;
It is so sad and beautiful,
So tremulously like a dream.

(viii)

TO A SLENDER WIND

Chrysolith thy step,
And on a jewelled pool
Faint arrowy moonstone on a tear-culled cadence,

[225]

Like fragmentary rain
Shaken silkily from star-scaled boughs.

Each note of thy dusky song
Is a petal that has delicate breath
And is azure;
And is more beautiful than the drift of leaves.

(ix)

THE ELM

They are all goddesses;
Nodding like flowers,
They are further and more delicate
Than the years that dwindle;
They are deeper in darkness
Than the hours.

Celestial,
Slenderly lethal things,
Beautifully little like clouds:
Leaf driftwood that has blown.

(x)

THE OAK

Fierce colours ned about the branches,
Enveloping the ragged leaves unseen and strewn.

Hazardous reflections dipped in evening
Hover, making the forest fluctuantly vague.

Something austere hides, something uncertain
Beneath the deep bark calls and makes quiet music.

THE PINE

Virgate and sprung of the dusk,
The pine is the tree of the breeze,
And the winds that stream through the ribboned light
And the motley winds from the seas.

TO THE SPRING-SPIRIT

And when it was spring I said,
  'Linger not deeper in the coloured trees,
But beautifully flake your head
  With foam flung by the flowering seas.'

And you arose from depths of grass
  That whispered with the wind and wept,
Saying you would let the chill seas pass,
  Seeking no further than your petals that still slept.

And I forgot the driftless foam, and sand,
  Idling with the radiance of the hours
Among the quiet trees. And hand in hand
  We strangely sang among the feathery flowers.

TRIOLET

The bees are glad the livelong day,
For lilacs in their beauty blow
And make my garden glad and gay.

The bees are glad the livelong day,
They to my blossoms wing their way,
And honey steal from flowers aglow.
The bees are glad the livelong day,
For lilacs in their beauty blow.

(xiv)

YOU SHALL NOT DESPAIR

You shall not despair
Because I have forsaken you
Or cast your love aside;
There is a greater love than mine
Which can comfort you
And touch you with softer hands.
I am no longer
Friendly and beautiful to you;
Your body cannot gladden me,
Nor the splendour of your dark hair,
But I do not humiliate you;
You shall be taken sweetly again
And soothed with slow tears;
You shall be loved enough.

(xv)

MY RIVER

My river, even though it lifts
Ledges of waves high over your head,
Cannot wear your edge away,
Round it so smoothly,
Or rub your bright stone.

You stand a little apart,
Strong enough to tread on the sand
And leave a clear print,
Strong and beautiful enough
To thrust your arm into the earth
And leave a tunnel
Looking up at you.
The metallic rain
Cannot dent your flanks;
The wind cannot blunt
The blade of your long foot,
Nor can the snow
Smooth the prisms of your breasts.
Sea, do not flow
Against this side.

You stretch out your hands
To touch the hydrangeas,
Then take them away quickly
As the mouth of the tiger-lily
Closes about your clasped fingers
With uneven, spiral teeth.
Your hands are beautiful hands
With slender fingers
And milk-white nails.
Your eyes can be the eyes
Of the nightingale,
Or the eyes of the eagle
Rising on black wings.
Your voice can be the voice
Of the sea under the hard sun,
The sea speaking keenly,
Or the voice of the river
Moving in one direction,
In a pattern like a shell
Lying upon the yellow beach.

My river cannot rub your bright stone,
Which cuts into the strength
And takes the heat away.
My river has high waves,
But your stone is many pointed,
And your side is steep.

(xvi)

WE WILL BE CONSCIOUS OF OUR SANCTITY

We will be conscious of our sanctity
That ripens as we develop
Our rods and substantial centres,
Our branches and holy leaves
On the edge beyond your reach;
We will remark upon the size
Of our roots,
Beautiful roots
Because they are under the surface
Of our charm.
Give us the pleasure of regret;
Our tears sound wiser
Than our laughter at the air
Or the yellow linnet who does not merit it.
We will be conscious of our divinity
When the time comes,
Unashamed but not with delight,
Making our affections fast;
We will tie you down
To one sense of finality
Like a cave with one thread.
Under this shade
The kingfisher comes

And the fresh-water bird
With his pink beak,
But we do not concern ourselves,
Waiting, waiting,
Waiting for the bird who shall say,
'I have come to elevate you,
To saw through your roots
And let you float.'
Then will we rise
Upon broad wings
And go into the air,
Burrow our way upwards into the blue sky;
This shade
Has the dragonfly and the swordfish
Cleaving their own sedges,
The otter
Hand in hand with the mermaid
Creeping catlike under the water.
We will be conscious
Of a new country
Opening in the blind cloud over our heads;
We will be conscious of a great divinity
And a wide sanity

(xvii)

I HAVE COME TO CATCH YOUR VOICE

I have come to catch your voice,
Your constructed notes going out of the throat
With dry, mechanical gestures,
To catch the shaft
Although it is so straight and unbending;
Then, when I open my mouth,

The light will come in an unwavering line.
Then to catch night
Wading through her dark cave on ferocious wings.
Oh, eagle-mouthed,
I have come to pluck you,
And take away your exotic plumage,
Although your anger is not a slight thing,
Take you into my own place
Where the frost can never fall,
Nor the petals of any flower drop.

(xviii)

WHEN YOUR FURIOUS MOTION

When your furious motion is steadied,
And your clamour stopped,
And when the bright wheel of your turning voice is stilled,
Your step will remain about to fall.
So will your voice vibrate
And its edge cut the surface,
So, then, will the dark cloth of your hair
Flow uneasily behind you.

This ponderous flower
Which leans one way,
Weighed strangely down upon you
Until you could bear it no longer
And bent under it,
While its violet shells broke and parted.
When you are gone
The scent of the great flower will stay,
Burning its sweet path clearer than before.
Press, press, and clasp steadily;

You shall not let go;
Chain the strong voice
And grip the inexorable song,
Or throw it, stone by stone,
Into the sky.

(xix)

NO THOUGHT CAN TROUBLE MY UNWHOLESOME POSE

No thought can trouble my unwholesome pose,
Nor make the stern shell of my spirit move.
You do not hurt, nor can your hand
Touch to remember and be sad.
I take you to myself, sweet pain,
And make you bitter with my cold,
My net that takes to break
The fibres, or the senses' thread.
No love can penetrate
The thick hide covering,
The strong, unturning crust that hides
The flower from the smell,
And does not show the fruit to taste;
No wave comb the sea,
And settle in the steady path.
Here is the thought that comes
Like a bird in its lightness,
On the sail of each slight wing
White with the rising water.
Come, you are to lose your freshness.
Will you drift into the net willingly,
Or shall I drag you down
Into my exotic composure?

NO, PIGEON, I'M TOO WISE

No, pigeon, I'm too wise;
No sky for me that carries
Its shining clouds for you;
Sky has not loved me much,
And if it did, who should I have
To wing my shoulders and my feet?
There's no way.
Ah, nightingale, my voice
Could never touch your spinning notes,
Nor be so clear.
I'm not secure enough
To tell what note I could reach if I tried,
But no high tree for me
With branches waiting for a singing bird,
And every nightingale a swan
Who sails on tides of leaves and sound.
I'm all for ground,
To touch what's to be touched,
To imitate myself mechanically,
Doing my little tricks of speech again
With all my usual care.
No bird for me:
He flies too high.

WOMAN ON TAPESTRY

Her woven hands beckoned me,
And her eyes pierced their intense love into me,
And I drew closer to her
Until I felt the rhythm of her body

Like a living cloak over me.
I saw the cold, green trees,
Their silken branches unmoving,
Their delicate, silken leaves folded,
And the deep sky over them
With immeasurable sadness.

Her love for me is fierce and continual,
Strong, fresh, and overpowering.
My love for her is like the moving of a cloud
Serene and unbroken,
Or the motion of a flower
Stirring its pole stem in delight,
Or the graceful sound of laughter.
In the victory of her gladness
And the triumph of her pitiless gaiety
She became like a dancer or a pretty animal
Suave in her movements,
On the balance of her dark foot,
Stepping down.

Let me believe in the clean faith of the body,
The sweet, glowing vigour
And the gestures of unageing love.
She shall make for me
A sensitive confusion in the blood,
A rhythm I cannot break
Stroking the air and holding light.

And the roots of the trees climbed through the air
Touching the silver clouds,
Trailing their fingers on the hard edges
Pacing in kind praise.

I have made an image of her
With the power of my hands

And the cruelty of my subtle eyes,
So that she appears entertaining
Like the arms of a clean woman
Or the branches of a green tree.

Death comes to the beautiful.
He is a friend with fresh breath
And small, feminine shoulders,
And white, symmetrical lips
Drawing the energy from the love,
And the glitter from the fine teeth.

You shall comfort me
With your symmetrical devotion
And the web of your straight senses.
Your bitterness is masked with smiles,
And your sharp pity is unchangeable.
I can detect a tolerance,
A compassion springing from the deep body,
Which goes around me easily
Like the body of a girl.
So the ilex and the cypress
Mix their wild blood
With yours,
And thrill and breathe and move
Unhealthily with dry veins.

There will be a new bitterness
Binding me with pain,
And a clean surge of love moving.
In the fold of her arms
And the contact with her breasts
There will be a new life
Growing like a powerful root inside me.
The gestures of my love
Involve me in a gaiety,

[236]

Recall my old desire
Like a sweet, sensitive plant
In the barbed earth,
Holding a voluptuous clarity
Under the tent of its wings.

So the hills
Coiled into their bodies like snakes,
And the trees
Went away from the bright place.

Let me believe in the clean faith of the body,
The sweet, glowing vigour,
And the gestures of unageing love.

(xxii)

PILLAR BREAKS

Pillar breaks, and mast is cleft
Now that the temple's trumpeter
Has stopped, (angel, you're proud),
And gallantly (water, you're strong—
You batter back my fleet),
Boat cannot go.

The raven's fallen and the magpie's still.
Silly to cage and then set free,
You loose, delicious will
That teaches me to wait,
Whose minute kindles more than the wise hour.
Temple should never have been filled
With ravens beating on the roof:
One day they had to fly,

[237]

And, there, what wings they had,
Poor, broken webs to strike the sky!
It was the magpie, after,
Bird on the mast, (he contemplated),
Who flew himself because the boat remained
Unmoving in a shouldering sea,
Flew for a time in vain, to drop at last
And catch the uprising wave.

Pity is not enough:
Temple's broken and poor raven's dead;
Build from the ashes!
Boat's broken, too, and magpie's still;
Build, build again!

(xxiii)

IT'S LIGHT THAT MAKES THE INTERVALS

It's light that makes the intervals
Between the pyramids so large,
And shows them fair against the dark,
Light that compels
The yellow bird to show his colour.
Light, not so to me;
Let me change to blue,
Or throw a violet shadow when I will.
To-day, if all my senses act,
I'll make your shape my own,
Grow into your delicate skin,
Feel your woman's breasts rise up like flowers
And pulse to open
Your wide smile for me.
Challenge my metamorphosis,

And I will break your spacing light.
Mock me,
And see your colour snap,
Glass to my hands endowed with double strength.
But if you break I suffer,
There'll be my bone to go:
Oh, let me destroy for once,
Rend the bright flesh away,
And twine the limbs around my hands.
I never break but feel the sudden pain,
The ache return.
I'll have to break in thought again,
Crush your sharp light,
And chip, in silence and in tears,
Your rock of sound.

(xxiv)

LET ME ESCAPE

Let me escape,
Be free, (wind for my tree and water for my flower),
Live self for self,
And drown the gods in me,
Or crush their viper heads beneath my foot.
No space, no space, you say,
But you'll not keep me in
Although your cage is strong.
My strength shall sap your own;
I'll cut through your dark cloud
To see the sun myself,
Pale and decayed, an ugly growth.

THE ROD CAN LIFT ITS TWINING HEAD

The rod can lift its twining head
To maim or sting my arm,
But if it stings my body dead
I'll know I'm out of harm,
For death is friendly to the man
Who lets his own rod be
The saviour of the cross who can
Compel eternity.
I'd rather have the worm to feed
Upon my flesh and skin,
Than sit here wasting, while I bleed,
My aptitude for sin.

(xxvi)

ADMIT THE SUN

Admit the sun into your high nest
Where the eagle is a strong bird
And where the light comes cautiously
To find and then to strike;
Let the frost harden
And the shining rain
Drop onto your wings,
Bruising the tired feathers.

I build a fortress from a heap of flowers;
Wisdom is stored with the clove
And the head of the bright poppy.
I bury, I travel to find pride
In the age of Lady Frankincense
Lifting her smell over the city buildings.

Where is there greater love
For the muscular and the victorious
Than in the gull and the fierce eagle
Who do not break?

Take heed of strength!
It is a weapon that can turn back
From the well-made hand
Out of the air it strikes.

A PUB POEM

(*Untitled*)

Sooner than you can water milk or cry Amen
Darkness comes, psalming, over Cards again;
Some lights go on; some men go out; some men slip in;
Some girls lie down, calling the beer-brown bulls to sin
And boom among their fishy fields; some elders stand
With thermoses and telescopes and spy the sand
Where farmers plough by night and sailors rock and rise,
Tattooed with texts, between the Atlantic thighs
Of Mrs Rosser Tea and little Nell the Knock:
One pulls out *Pam in Paris* from his money sock;
One from the mothy darkness of his black back house
Drinks vinegar and paraffin and blinds a mouse;
One reads his cheque book in the dark and eats fish-heads;
One creeps into the Cross Inn and fouls the beds;
One in the rubbered hedges rolls with a bald Liz
Who's old enough to be his mother (and she is);
Customers in the snugbar by the gobgreen logs
Tell other customers what they do with dogs;
The chemist is performing an unnatural act
In the organ loft; and the lavatory is packed.

NOTES

A NOTE ON VERSE-PATTERNS

Though Thomas never entirely abandoned the orthodox metrical form of English verse, based on the position of stressed and unstressed syllables, he gradually used it less often in his later work, except in satire and occasional poems. A system based on syllabic count without regular stress pattern eventually took its place in his most serious poetry. He also experimented for a time with free verse, that is, verse liberated from pattern, or at least from a set pattern.

Each of these three types of verse-pattern predominates at different times. The periods overlap, and characteristics of one period persist and recur, but in spite of this, chronological division gives a clear picture, if not a perfectly accurate one.

The earliest poems—that is, the poems of Thomas's boyhood—are, not unexpectedly, essays in traditional patterns of metre and stanza-structure. The Swinburnian or Meredithian line, with its big feet tripping over one another, occurs often, but Thomas, like others, found it difficult to handle and unrewarding in its effect, and soon came to prefer a more natural verse-beat, with weak stresses limited usually to one only in every foot. The anapaests recur later as a set pattern in only one poem, 'The sun burns the morning' (no. 69). During this period of apprenticeship, Thomas tried his hand at many strict forms of verse-structure, for example, the triolet (no. xiii). Writing about his dying father in what was to be almost his last poem, Thomas significantly chose once more to submit to the discipline of a strict form, the villanelle ('Do not go gentle into that good night', no. 162).

Influenced by several contemporary or near-contemporary poets, and affected by prevailing fashion, Thomas soon turned from conventional verse-patterns to so-called 'free verse'. The 1930 *Buffalo Notebook* bears the title: 'Mainly Free Verse Poems'.

The only possible definition of 'free verse' seems to be the negative one: verse without a set pattern. If a set pattern is allowed to intrude casually, that is, without some deliberate purpose, the medium is, as it were, violated. This happens, for example, when a weak-strong beat is maintained in several successive lines. To avoid this impression of uniformity, poets practising free verse made considerable use of logaoedic and speech rhythms, and when they were successful, the result can neither be mistaken for regular metrical verse nor be regarded as metrical anarchy. Free verse, indeed, is not only difficult: it is far from free. Perhaps the expression 'free verse' should be reserved for the failures; 'cadenced verse' is more appropriate to the successes.

These comments are necessary in order to explain the dissatisfaction with 'free verse' which Thomas soon felt, in common with many of his contemporaries. Free verse offered no help to a poet; with every line, every word, his was the full responsibility for turning it into 'cadenced verse'. The weak-strong beat, perhaps natural to the language, or perhaps instilled by reading of the literature, asserted itself unavoidably in long passages.

The most favoured substitute was equivalence (Coleridge) or sprung rhythm (Hopkins), a regular pattern imposed on the strong stresses, while the weak stresses (Coleridge) or the weaker stresses (Hopkins) are regarded as free. In spite of the influence of Hopkins on Thomas in other ways, this was not the system which Thomas chose to replace 'free verse'. Surprisingly, perhaps, he returned to traditional metre, but with a much greater skill and freedom than before. Cross-rhythms were overlaid upon the basic pattern to produce an effect of verse-counterpoint. Rhymes returned, but they were now in the form of half-rhymes. This was the only fashionable device Thomas retained, and he found good use for it in much of his remaining work. In spite of this, he was able to make fun of the half-rhyme:

> 'Do not forget that "limpet" rhymes
> With "strumpet" in these troubled times.'
>> ('A Letter to my Aunt', no. 79.)

Thomas eventually worked out a very complex technique of combining full rhymes, half-rhymes, assonances and alliterations. A suggestion of this will be found in the comparatively early poem 'Take the needles and the knives' (no. 66).

With the growth of his individuality in style and imagery, however, Thomas felt more and more strongly that conventional metre, even when treated 'contrapuntally', was inadequate for his needs. Those needs seemed contradictory: perfect flexibility, controlled by rigid discipline. The solution was provided by the system based on syllabic count, without regular stress pattern. This system, regularly adopted in the literatures of many foreign languages that have weak stresses, has appeared only occasionally in English literature, with its strong stresses. There are suggestions of syllabic count in 'The Litanie' and some other poems of Donne, and it emerges clearly as a system in the prophetic books of Blake, for example, in 'The Book of Thel', with its irregular stress-patterns within an almost regular syllabic count of fourteen. In the present century many poets have sought and found individual solutions for the verse-pattern problem; some have found the solution in equivalence or sprung rhythm, some in reversion to a modified conventional structure, and others—a small minority, it seems—in the 'syllabic count'. These include, for example, Marianne Moore (e.g. 'In Distrust of Merits': basic pattern, 9.9.8.10.10.7.7.7.6) and Herbert Read (e.g. 'Beata l'Alma': basic pattern, 9.6.7.2.12).

The first instance of Thomas's use of the syllabic count system is apparently 'I dreamed my genesis', written in November or early December, 1934 (no. 94); the count of 12, 7, 10, and 8 syllables is sustained, with only two irregular lines out of twenty-eight. This technique gave Thomas the flexibility and the discipline he needed, and it became predominant in his most serious and mature work.

Donne, perhaps, was Thomas's guide in the use of verse-patterns. Similarly, Donne and the 'metaphysical' poets influenced him in the structure of stanzas. The geometrical shapes of poems like 'Now, Say nay' (no. 109) and 'Vision and Prayer' (no. 149) make these poems too obvious as examples. 'Over Sir John's Hill' (no. 159) is more subtle as an illustration. The structure is reminiscent of the 'metaphysical' poets—for example, Traherne—in many ways: the size of the stanza, its elaborate pattern, the combination of lines differing greatly in length, the inclusion of lines unusually long (fifteen syllables) and unusually short (one syllable), and the relation of lines of contrasting length to one another by rhyme or similar means. The lines are of the following syllabic length: 5, 6, 14 (13), 14 (15), 5 (4, 6), 1, 13 (14, 15), 5 (4, 6), 14 (13), and 13 (14). (The figures in brackets are variants.) The patterns of the endings may be represented by the letters a a b c c b x d a d x x. The letters a, b, c, d, are full rhymes or half-rhymes. The two-syllable endings indicated by x are more subtly related; they alliterate, and at the same time are connected by assonance in the first syllable only: hedges, heron, headstone; paddles, passage, prancing; dilly, dingle, distant; whistles, windows, whispering; scaly, shaken, sailing. There are also connections between words by alliteration or assonance within the line too complex to analyse here. This poem, one of the last completed by Thomas, is fully representative of the verse technique of his mature writing.

It could be argued that some of the verse-patterns of Thomas, while accompanying certain perceptible impressions, produce no impressions that can be directly ascribed to the patterns alone, and that from this standpoint they are artificial devices and abstract conceptions. What human ear, it might be asked, could detect that the ending of the third line of 'Prologue' rhymes with another ending sixty-eight lines later? With less justice, in my opinion, the syllabic-count system might be criticized on the grounds that, even if it is perceptible as a numerical pattern, it is easily overcome by the natural patterns of the English language, based upon combinations of weak and strong stresses. For example, the syllabic-count equality of the following two lines (fourteen) would appear to such critics to be entirely lost in the unequal beat of the strong stresses (five and at least six):

'And green and golden I was huntsman and herdsman, the calves
Sang to my horn, the foxes on the hills barked clear and cold.'

('Fern Hill', no. 156.)

The criticism of the syllabic-count system depends upon

individual reading and perception; that is to say, it may be true for some readers, but it is certainly not true for all. There is also an answer to the general accusation of 'artificiality'. The artist, when faced with an infinite number of possibilities, is quite powerless; for example, the painter requires a framework, the composer a tone-row or some other convention, and the poet a planned structure. Within his self-imposed discipline, the artist can begin work.

In this Note, emphasis has necessarily been placed on verse-technique, as if it were an element detachable from the poetry itself. It is, in fact, detachable only in analysis, not in synthesis. To counterbalance this impression, I end with a quotation from the modern Greek poet Kazantzakis (in Kimon Friar's translation): 'A verse is not a garment with which one dresses one's emotion in order to create song; both verse and emotion are created in a momentary flash, inseparably, just as a man himself is created, body and soul, as one being.'

The dates of first publication of the principal volumes of Thomas's poems were:

December 1934 (*Eighteen Poems*)
Tenth September 1936 (*Twenty-five Poems*)
Twenty-fourth August 1939 (*The Map of Love*)
Seventh February 1946 (*Deaths and Entrances*) and
Tenth November 1952 (*Collected Poems*).

The figure following *Collected Poems* indicates the position of the poem in that book.

The words *Buffalo Notebook* may be misleading. There are in fact four poetry Notebooks in the Lockwood Memorial Library, Buffalo, N.Y., dated (1) 27th April 1930–9th December 1930; (2) December 1930–1st July 1932; (3) 1st February 1933–16th August 1933, and (4) 17th August 1933– 30th April 1934. It will be obvious from the context which of the four Notebooks is intended. Once again I should like to express my indebtedness to Professor Ralph Maud, whose *Poet in the Making* was invaluable in establishing the dates of composition of many of the poems written during the period covered by the Notebooks.

Prologue. August 1952. Written specially for *Collected Poems* (10th November 1952), this poem was enclosed in a letter to E. F. Bozman dated 10th September 1952 (*Selected Letters*, p. 376). About the form of the Prologue, reminiscent of the most abstruse experiments of the Provençal and mediaeval Welsh poets, Thomas writes: 'I set myself, foolishly perhaps, a most difficult technical task: The Prologue is in two verses—in my manuscript, a verse to a page—of 51 lines each. And the second verse rhymes *backward* with the first. The first & last lines of the poem rhyme; the second and the last but one; & so on & so on. Why I acrosticked myself like this, don't ask me.'

POEMS 1–163

1. Dated November 3rd (1930) in the *Buffalo Notebook*. There

is no indentation in the original. Four of the lines, however, begin without a capital letter, and in my view there are structural reasons for indenting them.

2. November 1930. The date can be conjectured from the *Buffalo Notebook*. Text in British Museum Add. MSS. 48217.

3. November 1930. The date can be conjectured from the *Buffalo Notebook*. Text in British Museum Add. MSS. 48217.

4. Dated 22nd November 1930 in the *Buffalo Notebook*. The text here is as in British Museum Add. MSS. 48217; but, following the suggestion of Professor Maud (*Poet in the Making*, p. 287), I have changed the original 'my' in line 15 to 'her'.

5. Dated 19th December 1930 in the *Buffalo Notebook*. Text in British Museum Add. MSS. 48217.

6. Dated 2nd January 1931 in the *Buffalo Notebook*. Text in British Museum Add. MSS. 48217.

7. Dated 20th January 1931 in the *Buffalo Notebook*. Text in British Museum Add. MSS. 48217.

8. Dated 27th January 1931 in the *Buffalo Notebook*. The text given here is the revised version quoted in a letter to Vernon Watkins (13th November 1937, *Letters to Vernon Watkins*, p. 31) and later published in *Wales* IV, March 1938, p. 138, with the title 'Poem'. In the letter Thomas implies that 'The spire cranes' is a new poem: 'since writing this, I've done another little poem.' The revision, however, was not significant, and the date 1931 seems preferable. (*Collected Poems* no. 50.)

9. Dated February 24th (1931) in the *Buffalo Notebook*. Line 8: the original has a full stop, for which I have substituted a comma.

10. Dated March 1931 in the *Buffalo Notebook*. The poem occurs out of order, between poems dated October and November.

11. Dated 30th March 1931 in the *Buffalo Notebook*. Text in British Museum Add. MSS. 48217.

12. Dated March 20th (1931) in the *Buffalo Notebook*. Line 6: the original has a full stop, for which I have substituted a comma.
13. Dated 6th April 1931 in the *Buffalo Notebook*. Text in British Museum Add. MSS. 48217.
14. Dated 10th April 1931 in the *Buffalo Notebook*.
15. Dated June 1st 1931 in the *Buffalo Notebook*. As in some other poems written at about the same time, the absence of punctuation at the end of the poem seems to be intentional (see Note (xvi)).
16. Dated June 1st 1931 in the *Buffalo Notebook*; apparently written immediately after no. 15.
17. Dated August 12th 1931 in the *Buffalo Notebook*.
18. Dated August 16th (1931) in the *Buffalo Notebook*. As in nos. 15 and (xvi), the absence of punctuation at the end of the poem seems to be intentional.
19. Dated 18th August 1931 in the *Buffalo Notebook*. Text in British Museum Add. MSS. 48217.
20. August 1931. This occurs in the *Buffalo Notebook* between poems dated 18th August and 11th September. A neater copy, with the difference of a comma, appears later in the Notebook with the date 10th October, but the earlier date is evidently the date of composition.
21. Dated 24th September 1931 in the *Buffalo Notebook*. Text in British Museum Add. MSS. 48217.
22. Dated 17th October 1931 in the *Buffalo Notebook*.
23. Dated October 26th (1931) in the *Buffalo Notebook*. The array of negatives, grammatical or otherwise, is intentional, as the whole poem shows (e.g. line 4).
24. Dated October (1931) in the *Buffalo Notebook*.
25. Dated 20th January 1932 in the *Buffalo Notebook*. Text in British Museum Add. MSS. 48217.
26. Dated April 1932 in the *Buffalo Notebook*. Text in British Museum Add. MSS. 48217.
27. April 1932. This poem was addressed to James Chapman Woods, a Swansea poet, and it appeared with an article on him by Thomas in *The Herald of Wales*, 23rd April 1932.

28. Dated May 7th 1932 in the *Buffalo Notebook*. I have supplied a comma in the last line after 'men', as in the first line.

29. Dated June 7th 1932 in the *Buffalo Notebook*. First published in *Twenty-five Poems*, pp. 17–18. (*Collected Poems* no. 27.)

30. Dated June 25th 1932 in the *Buffalo Notebook*. A full stop has been supplied after 'rhythms' in the penultimate line.

No. 5 Cwmdonkin Drive, Swansea, where Thomas lived, was in a row of houses occupying one side only of a very steep road. Immediately opposite were the grounds of a private school, Clevedon College, overlooked by a stand of tall conifers. In term time, many a crazy game of football could be seen from Thomas's front windows, the toss-winners enjoying at least seventy-five degrees' advantage in their headlong attack. At other times, the field was full of bronchial sheep who did nothing but cough.

Line 18: The foundations of Cefn Coed Hospital were laid in 1929, not far from Cwmdonkin Drive, but the hospital was not opened for patients until 8th December 1932. At the time when this poem was written, therefore, the enormous building was standing high on one of Swansea's many hills, empty, but ready.

31. Autumn 1932. The date is conjectured from the position of the poem in British Museum Add. MSS. 48217.

32. Autumn 1932. The date is conjectured from the position of the poem in British Museum Add. MSS. 48217.

33. Autumn 1932. The date is conjectured from the position of the poem in British Museum Add. MSS. 48217.

34. Autumn 1932. The date is conjectured from the position of the poem in British Museum Add. MSS. 48217.

35. Autumn 1932. The date is conjectured from the position of the poem in British Museum Add. MSS. 48217.

36. Autumn 1932. The date is conjectured from the position of the poem in British Museum Add. MSS. 48217.

37. Autumn 1932. The date is conjectured from the position of the poem in British Museum Add. MSS. 48217.

38. Dated February 6th 1933 in the *Buffalo Notebook*.

39. Dated 8th February 1933 in the *Buffalo Notebook*. First published in *The New English Weekly*, IX, 16, p. 310, 30th July 1936, with the title 'Poem'. (*Collected Poems* no. 29.)

40. The first three stanzas are dated February 16th 1933 in the *Buffalo Notebook*; the poem was finished on the following day.

   The original position of the inverted commas has been kept; this gives the first stanza the effect of a text or a quotation which is elaborated in the rest of the poem. At the same time, it is tempting to place the inverted commas elsewhere, for example, in stanza I, 'We who are young are old', and, in stanza II, 'We who are still young are old', or to omit the inverted commas altogether, in order to make stanzas I, II and VI consistent with one another.

   In the 6th line of stanza V, a hyphen has been supplied where the original has 'Exsoldiers'.

41. Dated 22nd February 1933 in the *Buffalo Notebook*.

42. No date given, but the position of the poem in the *Buffalo Notebook* suggests that it was written towards the end of February 1933.

43. Dated 1st March 1933 in the *Buffalo Notebook*. First published in *New Verse*, XVIII, pp. 16–17, December 1935, and included with slight revision in *Twenty-five Poems*, p. 35. (*Collected Poems* no. 38.)

44. Dated 28th March 1933 in the *Buffalo Notebook*.

45. Dated 28th March 1933 in the *Buffalo Notebook*.

46. Dated 31st March 1933 in the *Buffalo Notebook*. First published in *The Herald of Wales*, VI, 746, p. 1, 8th June 1935, and quoted by Thomas in his broadcast 'Reminiscences of Childhood' (*The Listener*, 25th February 1943, pp. 246–7; *Quite Early One Morning*, pp. 1–7).

47. Dated 1st April 1933 in the *Buffalo Notebook*.

48. Dated April 1933 in the *Buffalo Notebook*. First published, with revision principally in the form of omissions, in *The New English Weekly*, 18th May 1933. (*Collected Poems* no. 41.)

49. Dated 16th–20th April 1933 in the *Buffalo Notebook*. First

published in *The New English Weekly*, IV, 15, pp. 342–3, 25th January 1934. Line 26, Sanger: 'Lord' John Sanger, famous nineteenth-century impresario.

50. Dated 16th May 1933 in the *Buffalo Notebook*. First published, with some revision and condensation, in *Poetry, Chicago*, XLIX, 4, p. 183, January 1937. (*Collected Poems* no. 47.)

51. Dated 23rd May 1933 in the *Buffalo Notebook*. First published in *Adelphi*, VI, 6, p. 398, 6th September 1933.

52. Dated 1st July 1933 in the *Buffalo Notebook*. First published, slightly revised, as the first of 'Two Poems', in *The New English Weekly*, IX, 14, p. 270, 16th July 1936. (*Collected Poems* no. 31.)

53. Dated 7th July 1933 in the *Buffalo Notebook*. First published in *The Herald of Wales*, 15th July 1933. There were two open-air performances of Sophocles' *Electra* at Mrs Bertie Perkins's house on Sketty Green, Swansea, for which, by the way, I wrote music for harp and drums. Thomas refers to this poem in 'Return Journey', broadcast on 15th June 1947 (see *Quite Early One Morning*). These performances made a strong impression on the poet at the time. See, for example, 'The Woman Speaks' (no. 59).

54. This follows 'Greek Play in a Garden' in the *Buffalo Notebook*, and is given the same date of composition, July 7th 1933. The word 'pome', used in line 11, may have originated in Joyce's *Pomes Penyeach* (1927), but I cannot recall and do not think that it did. It was a jocular version of the word 'poem' often used by Thomas and his friends, sometimes satirically, as here, but more often with a kind of affectionate informality. 'Pomes' were, of course, written by 'potes' and bound into almost wafer-thin volumes of 'potry'.

55. Dated 9th July 1933 in the *Buffalo Notebook*. First published, with some revision, in *Twenty-five Poems*, p. 14. (*Collected Poems* no. 25.)

56. Dated July 14th 1933 in the *Buffalo Notebook*.

57. Dated 15th July 1933 in the *Buffalo Notebook*. First pub-

lished, with deletions, in *Purpose*, VIII, 2, pp. 102–3, April 1936. (*Collected Poems* no. 39.)

58. Dated 17th July 1933 in the *Buffalo Notebook*. First published, with deletion, in *John O'London's Weekly*, 5th May 1934. The full version appeared in *Collected Poems* (no. 34).

59. Dated July 1933 in the *Buffalo Notebook*. Text in British Museum Add. MSS. 48217. First published in *Adelphi*, VII, 6, pp. 399–400, March 1934, with this title. The original title, 'From a Play to be called "Ravens"', suggests a connection between the poem and no. 53, 'Greek Play in a Garden'.

60. Dated August 1933 in the *Buffalo Notebook*. Published, with deletions, in *Twenty-five Poems*, p. 13. (*Collected Poems* no. 24.)

61. Dated 17th August 1933 in the *Buffalo Notebook*. First published, with the omission of the last stanza, in *New Verse*, XVIII, pp. 15–16, December 1935. (*Collected Poems* no. 36.)

62. Dated 20th August 1933 in the *Buffalo Notebook*. Dedicated to Trevor Hughes.

63. Dated 22nd August 1933 in the *Buffalo Notebook*.

64. Dated 6th September 1933 in the *Buffalo Notebook*. Text in British Museum Add. MSS. 48217. First published, with deletions, in *Eighteen Poems*, IV. (*Collected Poems* no. 4.)

65. Dated 8th September 1933 in the *Buffalo Notebook*. The poem is included here in spite of the disparaging remarks Thomas himself made about it in a letter to Pamela Hansford Johnson dated 2nd May 1934 (*Selected Letters*, p. 116).

66. Dated September 12th (1933) in the *Buffalo Notebook*.
    The versification is interesting in this poem. A simple and perfectly regular metrical pattern is combined here with a complex arrangement of endings. The stanzas should be taken in pairs. If capital letters represent assonances, small letters full rhymes and figures half-rhymes, a pair of stanzas follows the pattern: A a 1 a - B b 1 b. For example: stanza V, slayer, labour (the same first vowel), pain, sabre (full rhyme

with 'labour'); stanza VI, fire, viper (the same first vowel), machine (half-rhyme with 'pain'), sniper (full rhyme with 'viper'). At the same time, it must be admitted that this scheme is not carried out as consistently as the metrical scheme.

67. Dated 15th September 1933 in the *Buffalo Notebook*. Thomas intended to include a revised version of this poem in his first published book of poems (*Selected Letters*, p. 116).

68. Dated 16th September 1933 in the *Buffalo Notebook*. The text here is as in the first publication (*The New English Weekly*, IX, 16, p. 310, 30th July 1936).

69. Dated 16th September 1933 in the *Buffalo Notebook*. One of the last instances of deliberate anapaestic rhythm, recalling—in this alone, of course—some of Thomas's earliest poems.

70. Dated 17th September 1933 in the *Buffalo Notebook*. Text in British Museum Add. MSS. 48217. First published in *Eighteen Poems*, VI, 18th December 1934. (*Collected Poems* no. 6.)

71. Dated 18th September 1933 in the *Buffalo Notebook*. First published in the *Sunday Referee*, 7th January 1934, with this title.

72. Dated 30th September 1933 in the *Buffalo Notebook*.

73. Dated 12th October 1933 in the *Buffalo Notebook*. First published in the *Sunday Referee*, 29th October 1933. (*Collected Poems* no. 5.)

74. Dated 14th–17th October 1933 in the *Buffalo Notebook*. First published, with deletion at the end of the poem, in *Criterion*, XIV, 54, pp. 27–8, October 1934. (*Collected Poems* no. 12.)

75. Dated 16th October 1933 in the *Buffalo Notebook*, this follows most of the previous poem (no. 74) but precedes its completion.

76. Not dated, but the position of the poem in the *Buffalo Notebook* suggests that it was written between 17th and 25th October 1933. Professor Maud (*Poet in the Making*, p. 329)

points out that the ninth line of this poem reappears in 'I dreamed my genesis' (no. 94, line 9).

77. Dated 25th October 1933 in the *Buffalo Notebook*.

78. Dated 20th November 1933 in the *Buffalo Notebook*. Text in British Museum Add. MSS. 48217. First published, with very little revision but with the title 'Light', in *The Listener*, XI, 270, p. 462, 14th March 1934. (Without title, *Collected Poems* no. 14.)

79. November or December 1933. In a letter to Pamela Hansford Johnson (*Selected Letters*, p. 69). To appreciate the full flavour of these verses, it is necessary to know something of the circumstances in which they were written. In the summer of 1933 I met Victor Neuberg, Runia Tharp (no 'e' at the end, I think) and Pamela Hansford Johnson at Steyning; this was before Thomas knew them or knew of them. Miss Johnson, in a hammock, read passages from the manuscript of her poems, which were soon to appear as the first volume of the *Sunday Referee Poets Series*, published by Neuberg. Runia Tharp held forth about her theory that poetry and music should always be improvisatory; she found nothing inconsistent with that theory in the recording and the playing or reading of such improvisations over and over again. When I returned to Swansea, I told Thomas—in rather disparaging terms, I'm afraid—about my afternoon at Steyning. He absorbed the information quietly, and, about a week later (3rd September), his first *Sunday Referee* poem appeared: 'That sanity be kept' (see note 89). In this rather odd way Thomas began his progress towards recognition as a poet, and about a year later he became the second of the *Sunday Referee* poets to be published by Neuberg in book form (*Eighteen Poems*, December 1934). In spite of this, both Miss Johnson and Thomas recognized from the first the preciosity of the Neuberg circle. The satire of 'A Letter to my Aunt' has two targets; apart from the obvious one, Thomas aims a few shafts at himself, at his fondness for half-rhymes ('limpet', 'strumpet'), his obsession with the

charnel-house ('each rose is wormy') and his short flirtation with Surrealism, of which David G(ascoyne) was at this time chief London representative.

80. Dated 13th December 1933 in the *Buffalo Notebook*. Text in British Museum Add. MSS. 48217.

81. Dated 24th December 1933 in the *Buffalo Notebook*. First published as the second of 'Two Poems', in *The New English Weekly*, IX, 14, p. 270, 16th July 1936. (*Collected Poems* no. 20.) (See note 52.)

82. Dated 12th January 1934 in the *Buffalo Notebook*. The stanza form here is strikingly reminiscent of the Breconshire poet Henry Vaughan. Some readers may be interested in the influence of Welsh poets on the work of Thomas. I would like to remind them that Donne, though born in London, was of Welsh parentage. Herbert is a more doubtful instance, but the name, a common one in Wales, is very suggestive. Thomas's great-uncle, Gwilym Marles Thomas (7th April 1834–11th December 1879), was a famous poet and a famous man in his day. I have two volumes of his poetry, and in one of them (facing page 33) there is a picture of Pont Llandysul (Llandysul Bridge) which crosses the river Marles. Gwilym Marles Thomas adopted the name of this river as his nom-de-plume. Dylan Thomas and his sister Nancy were both given the name Marles (but in the spelling Marlais) as their middle names. This, perhaps, is the place where I should mention that the name 'Dylan' should be pronounced 'Dillan'. In the great mediaeval prose work, *The Mabinogion*, the name occurs with a circumflex over the 'y'. Those who persist in pronouncing it 'Dullan' should read first *The Mabinogion*, and afterwards, perhaps, Pope's couplet that begins: 'A little learning . . . .' If they are still not convinced, I can assure them that the poet himself, all his family and all his friends used this pronunciation: 'Dillan'. It would be idle to pretend that this is a common Christian name in Wales, but—for obvious reasons—it is becoming more popular. I believe that, apart from Dylan Thomas himself,

my own son—the poet's godson—was the first to be called Dylan perhaps for centuries. My great friend Vernon Watkins even felt it necessary to ask my permission to call one of his sons Dylan.

83. Dated 2nd February 1934 in the *Buffalo Notebook*. First published in the *Sunday Referee*, 11th February 1934. (*Collected Poems* no. 3.)

84. Dated March 1934 in the *Buffalo Notebook*. First published in *New Verse*, VIII, pp. 11–12, April 1934. (*Collected Poems* no. 9.)

85. Dated 18th March 1934 in the *Buffalo Notebook*. First published in the *Sunday Referee*, 25th March 1934. (*Collected Poems* no. 7.)

86. Dated April 1934 in the *Buffalo Notebook*. First published in *New Verse*, IX, pp. 8–9, June 1934. (*Collected Poems* no. 1.)

87. Dated April 1934 in the *Buffalo Notebook*. There was an earlier version, dated September 1933, but the resemblance is not close. First published in *Eighteen Poems*, XIII, December 1934. (*Collected Poems* no. 13.)

88. Dated 30th April 1934 in the *Buffalo Notebook*. First published in *New Verse*, X, pp. 8–9, August 1934. (*Collected Poems* no. 8.)

89. June 1934. An earlier version of this poem was published in the *Sunday Referee* on 3rd September of the same year. The poem was considerably revised early in June 1934, and in this new form published in the *Swansea and West Wales Guardian*, 8th June 1934.

90. June 1934. This is the date of first publication in *New Verse*, IX, pp. 6–8, June 1934. Though based on an earlier poem sent to Pamela Hansford Johnson on 11th November 1933 (*Selected Letters*, p. 66), this is essentially a new composition. (*Collected Poems* no. 2.)

91. October 1934. First published on the 24th of that month in *The Listener*, XII, 302, p. 691. (*Collected Poems* no. 10.)

92. November or early December 1934. Written for inclusion in *Eighteen Poems* (XI). (*Collected Poems* no. 11.)

93. November or early December 1934. Written for inclusion in

Eighteen Poems (XV), this poem shows some resemblance to two earlier poems in the *Buffalo Notebook* dated October and November 1933, the second of which is in British Museum Add. MSS. 48217. (*Collected Poems* no. 15.)

94. November or early December 1934. Written for inclusion in *Eighteen Poems* (XVI). (*Collected Poems* no. 16.) This appears to be the first poem in which Thomas used the counting of syllables as the basis of his versification, without any fixed stress pattern. The lines consist of 12, 7, 10, and 8 syllables. Only lines 12 and 27 are irregular. At the end of line 4, a comma has been substituted for the original full stop.

95. November or early December 1934. Written for inclusion in *Eighteen Poems* (XVII), but first published, a few days before, in *New Verse*, XII, pp. 10–12. (*Collected Poems* no. 17.)

96. November or early December 1934. Written for inclusion in *Eighteen Poems* (XVIII). (*Collected Poems* no. 18.)

97. August 1935. This is the date of the final revision of the poem as it appears in the August 1933 *Buffalo Notebook*; two other poems in that notebook, dated August and September 1933, show some similarity, but August 1935 may be regarded as the date of composition. First published in *Comet*, I, 9, p. 66, 1s. February 1936. (*Collected Poems* no. 40.)

98. August–September 1935. This is the date of first publication in *New Verse*, XVI, pp. 2–5. (*Collected Poems* no. 19.) In Part II, line 17, a comma has been supplied after 'they', and in the next line, a comma has been substituted for the original semi-colon.

99. October 1935. This is the date of first publication in *The Scottish Bookman*, I, 2, p. 78. (*Collected Poems* no. 26.)

100. 23rd October 1935. This is the date of first publication in *Programme*, IX, pp. 2–3. (*Collected Poems* no. 33.)

101. 23rd October 1935. This is the date of first publication in *Programme*, IX, pp. 10–12. (*Collected Poems* no. 32.)

102. December 1935. This is the date of first publication in *New Verse*, XVIII, p. 16, as the second of three poems. (*Collected Poems* no. 37.) The other two, 'The hand that signed the

paper' and 'I have longed to move away', were written much earlier, the first on 17th August 1933 and the second on 1st March 1933. (See notes 61 and 43.)

103. December 1935. This is the date of publication of the first seven of these 'sonnets' in *Life and Letters To-day*, XIII, 2, pp. 73–5. The other three were written later, in 1936, when they were published in *Contemporary Poetry and Prose*, no. VIII in May, and nos. IX and X in July. The ten poems were brought together as a sequence in *Twenty-five Poems*, pp. 42–7. (*Collected Poems* no. 43.) The expression 'owl-light', by the way, was used by Webster in *The Duchess of Malfi* (IV, ii).

I consider this sequence to be a single poem in ten parts, perhaps unfinished. In my opinion, the theory put forward by Marshall W. Stearns ('Unsex the Skeleton', in *Transformation*, no. 3, 1946) that the sequence lacks continuity, and that it should be divided into separate poems, is plainly contradicted by the text itself. The plan of the whole poem was even larger than the ten sonnet-like stanzas Thomas finished. As Vernon Watkins says, 'He intended to write more and make it a much longer work' (*Letters to Vernon Watkins*, p. 13).

'Altarwise by owl-light' represents an important stage in the poet's development, and it has been the subject of literary controversy ever since its publication in *Twenty-five Poems*. The starting-point of the controversy was Edith Sitwell's review of the book and the subsequent correspondence in the *Sunday Times* (September 1936). In the review, which is warmly eulogistic, Edith Sitwell speaks of 'Altarwise by owl-light' as 'nothing short of magnificent, in spite of the difficulty'. This last phrase was seized upon by others and interpreted as an allegation of obscurity, in the ordinary sense of the word. Earlier in the same review, however, Edith Sitwell had made clear what she meant by 'difficulty': it was, she wrote, 'largely the result of the intense concentration of each phrase, packed with meaning, of the fusion (not confusion) of two profound thoughts'.

[262]

In spite of this, many 'interpretations' were offered; perhaps the most plausible was Francis Scarfe's reading of the poem as a mystical message conveyed by symbolism (*Auden and After*, pp. 106–10). At the other end of the scale there is Elder Olson's ludicrously complex decipherment based on astrology (*The Poetry of Dylan Thomas*, pp. 63–87). But Thomas himself insisted that 'Altarwise by owl-light' was not 'elliptical': 'this poem is a particular incident in a particular adventure' (*Sunday Times*, September 1936). In that statement, it would be wrong to substitute the word 'describes' for the word 'is'. At the same time, the 'being' of the poem is not abstraction; it has the solidity of purpose, continuity, and cohesion. Speaking of another poem (see Note 112), Thomas writes: 'Images *are* what they say, not what they stand for' (*Selected Letters*, p. 186). This statement, I suggest, should be interpreted similarly; images may not 'stand for' anything, but it is taken for granted that their existence includes purpose, effect, and inter-relation.

Poetry which aims at perfect abstraction relies on the connotation of words to the exclusion of their denotation; but, while words are used, it is impossible to escape from their denotation, and any attempt to produce 'absolute poetry' must either be less than absolute or must go beyond words and cease to be poetry. 'Altarwise by owl-light' lays great stress on connotation, as distinct from definition, and, without of course crossing the boundary set by the use of words, tends to move in that direction. It is a pattern of images and words, held together not by the logic of reason, narration or utility, but by the logic of a common relationship of those images and words with certain allied subjects: sex, birth, death, Christian and pagan religion and ritual. In other words, the poem sustains a single metaphor, and it would be vain to seek in it logic, narration or message in the usual sense of these words. Comprehension here is irrelevant. In the laboratory, crystals of distinctive form and colour may be dissolved, and, with the cooling of the solution will take on again forms and colours that are at least recognizable, if not identical. Unlike the chemical process, dissolution of such poetry as this, by 'translation' into other words, by 'interpretation into other thoughts', holds out no prospect of reversal to anything recognizable or even similar.

It remains true that 'Altarwise by owl-light' is 'difficult', because of the exceptionally dense concentration and complex interweaving of its imagery, and in this way it marks an important stage in the poet's development. Before this poem, Thomas had been moving towards greater extravagance in imagery; after it, he moved towards greater economy. In comparison with the almost claustrophobic denseness of 'Altarwise by owl-light', the later poems to an increasing degree create an effect of release and, as it were, 'ventilation'. But Thomas did not abandon the process of using a single sustained metaphor to achieve unity in a long poem; it became a recurrent characteristic of his writing. Here, as in many other ways, there is a parallel between Thomas's poetry and the work of Donne and the 'metaphysical' poets; his use of metaphor is an extension of their use of 'conceits'.

'In Country Heaven' (see Note 'a') remained unfinished, and we cannot tell whether that long poem, too, would have been held together by the 'sustained metaphor'; but it seems probable. As for Thomas's broadcast 'Introduction' to the poem, perhaps it was his memory of the reaction to 'Altarwise by owl-light' that prompted him to offer in advance some help to the reader, not to 'understand' 'In Country Heaven', but at least not to misunderstand his intentions in writing it.

104. 20th January 1936. This is the date of the final and considerably revised version of an earlier poem written on 16th May 1933. Both appear in the February 1933 *Buffalo Notebook*. The early version, not used here, was published in the *Sunday Referee* on 11th August 1935, with the title 'Poem for Sunday'. (*Collected Poems* no. 21.)

105. March 1936. This is the date of first publication in *Caravel*, *Majorca*, II, 5, p. 15. (*Collected Poems* no. 28.)

106. May 1936. This is the date of first publication in revised form. An early version in the *Buffalo Notebook* was dated February 1934 and published in the *Sunday Referee* on 28th October 1934. The poem was then almost entirely rewritten, and in its new form appeared in *Contemporary Poetry and Prose*, I, pp. 2–3, May 1936. (*Collected Poems* no. 35.)

107. 10th September 1936. This is the date of first publication in revised form. An early poem, dated in the *Buffalo Notebook* 18th December 1930, was thoroughly revised for publication in *Twenty-five Poems* (p. 9) and in effect became a new composition. (*Collected Poems* no. 22.)

108. 10th September 1936. This is the date of first publication in *Twenty-five Poems*, pp. 10–12. (*Collected Poems* no. 23.)

109. 10th September 1936. This is the date of first publication in *Twenty-five Poems*, pp. 21–2. (*Collected Poems* no. 30.)

110. 10th September 1936. This is the date of first publication in *Twenty-five Poems*, pp. 40–1. (*Collected Poems* no. 42.)

111. January 1937. This is the date of first publication in *Twentieth Century Verse*, I, p. 3. (*Collected Poems* no. 48.)

112. November 1937. Vernon Watkins, to whom this poem was sent on 13th November 1937, writes that it took roughly a year to finish (*Letters to Vernon Watkins*, p. 30). First published with the title: 'Poem (for Caitlin)' in *Twentieth Century Verse*, VIII, pp. 3–4. (*Collected Poems* no. 45.) Thomas very rarely attempted a prose analysis of a poem, but, when Hermann Peschmann wrote to him asking what 'I make this in a warring absence' is 'about', he did try to supply some kind of answer (*Selected Letters*, pp. 185–6). The warning to Mr Peschmann at the beginning of the letter is most significant (see Note to no. 103): 'I can give you a very rough idea of the "plot". But of course it's bound to be a most superficial, and perhaps misleading idea because the "plot" is told in images, and images *are* what they say, not what they stand for.' Here is Thomas's analysis: 'The poem

[265]

is, in the first place, supposed to be a document or narrative, of all the emotional events between the coming and going, the creation and dissipation, of jealousy, jealousy born from pride and killed by pride, between the absence and the return of the crucial character (or heroine) of the narrative, between the war of her absence and the armistice of her presence. The "I", the hero, begins his narrative at the departure of the heroine (Stanza One) at the time he feels that her pride in him and in their proud sexual world has been discarded.

'(Stanza Two) All that keen pride seems, to him, to have vanished, drawn back, perhaps, to the blind wound from which it came. (Stanza Three) He sees her as a woman made of contraries, innocent in guilt and guilty in innocence, ravaged in virginity, (Stanza Four) virgin in ravishment, and a woman who, out of weak coldness, reduces to nothing the great sexual strength, (Stanza Five) heats and prides of the world. Crying his visions aloud he makes war upon her absence, attacks and kills her absent heart, then falls, himself, into ruin at the moment of that murder of love. He falls into the grave: (Stanza Six) in his shroud he lies, empty of visions and legends; he feels undead love at his heart. The surrounding dead in the grave describe to him one manner of death and resurrection: (Stanza Seven) the womb, the origin of love, forks its child down to the dark grave, dips it in dust, then forks it back into light again. (Stanza Eight) And once in the light, the resurrected hero sees the world with penetrating, altered eyes; the world that·was wild is now mild to him, revenge has changed into pardon. (Stanza Nine) He sees his love walk in the world, bearing none of the murderous wounds he gave her. Forgiven by her, he ends his narrative forgiveness—but he sees and knows that all that has happened will happen again, tomorrow and tomorrow.'

Lines 37 and 38 were transposed in the original; this was apparently a mistake, and it is corrected here.

113. November 1937 is the date of this version in the February

1933 *Buffalo Notebook*. After extensive revision, a poem, written probably early in 1933, which appears in British Museum Add. MSS. 48217, reached this final form. First published, as the second of 'Four Poems', in *Poetry, Chicago*, LII, 5, August 1938. (*Collected Poems* no. 49.)

114. January 1938. An early poem, dated 20th April 1933 in the *Buffalo Notebook*, was transformed by considerable alteration and condensation into a new composition; this was sent to Vernon Watkins in March 1938 (*Letters to Vernon Watkins*, p. 37). First published in *Poetry, Chicago*, LII, 5, pp. 248–9, August 1938, as the third of 'Four Poems'. (*Collected Poems* no. 53.)

115. March 1938. The poem was sent to Vernon Watkins on that date (*Letters to Vernon Watkins*, p. 37). First published in *Criterion*, XVIII, 70, pp. 29–30, October 1938. (*Collected Poems* no. 54.)

116. Spring 1938. An earlier poem, dated 10th February 1933 in the *Buffalo Notebook*, was transformed by extensive revision into a new composition. The date of this revision is established by letters to Vernon Watkins (*Letters to Vernon Watkins*, pp. 37, 40, 57). The new text, with its present title, was first published in *Life and Letters To-day*, XVIII, 12, p. 45, Summer 1938. (*Collected Poems* no. 51.)

117. 16th June 1938. In a letter to Henry Treece (*Selected Letters*, p. 201). The poet Treece, though a great admirer of Thomas, caused him great annoyance in his book *Dylan Thomas, Dog among the Fairies*, published in 1949. Thomas's copy, which he gave me, is full of his angry annotations. It irritated him, for example, to be called 'Dylan' throughout, instead of 'Thomas', and he particularly disliked the chapter 'Is Dylan a Fake?' The 1938 letter was written, of course, long before their relationship deteriorated. 'Dog among the Fairies' is a quotation from a letter written to the *Sunday Times* by Thomas at the beginning of the 'Altarwise by owl-light' controversy (see Note no. 103).

118. August 1938. This is the date of first publication in *Poetry*,

Chicago, LII, 5, p. 247, as the first of 'Four Poems'. (*Col-lected Poems* no. 46.)

119. September 1938. Though this has some faint echoes in an earlier poem dated July 1933 in the *Buffalo Notebook*, this was sent as an entirely new composition to Vernon Watkins in September 1938 (*Letters to Vernon Watkins*, p. 43). The first publications show variants in the first line: '(Her) tombstone told (me) when she died'. First published in *Seven*, III, p. 17, Winter 1938. (*Collected Poems* no. 55.)

120. September 1938. A copy of the poem was sent to Vernon Watkins on this date (*Letters to Vernon Watkins*, p. 43). After some revision, it was first published in *Wales*, vi/vii, p. 196, in March 1939. (*Collected Poems* no. 56.)

121. October 1938. The poem was enclosed in a letter to Vernon Watkins dated 14th October 1938 (*Letters to Vernon Watkins*, p. 46). It was first published, with the title 'Poem', in *Seven*, III, October 1938, and not again published in the poet's lifetime.

122. October 1938. A copy of the poem was sent to Watkins on 14th October 1938 (*Letters to Vernon Watkins*, p. 44), and there is a reference to it in a letter to Henry Treece dated 16th October 1938 (*Selected Letters*, p. 214). First published in *Poetry, London*, I, pp. 26–7, February 1939. (*Collected Poems* no. 57.) On Henry Treece, see Note 117.

123. October 1938. Copied out on a postcard sent to Vernon Watkins on 24th October 1938, and written just before Thomas's twenty-fourth birthday (October 27th). He adds: 'This very short poem is for my birthday just arriving . . . I scrapped the poem beginning with that line long ago,' (Thomas is referring to the last line, 'I advance for as long as forever is'), 'and at last—I think—I've found the inevitable place for it: it was a time finding that place' (*Letters to Vernon Watkins*, pp. 47–8). First published in *Life and Letters To-day*, XX, 16, p. 42, December 1938. (*Collected Poems* no. 59.)

124. 16th November 1938. This parody of Frederic Prokosch's

poem 'The Dolls' is included in a letter to John Davenport of this date (*Selected Letters*, p. 217). It is a line-for-line distorted reflection of the original, but Thomas admitted that he could not quite do justice to the last line: 'Small tears of glass upon my bed'. Davenport and Thomas collaborated in writing an amusing murder story, *The Death of the King's Canary*, that is, the death of the Poet Laureate, in which many famous poets were the principal suspects. The novel is full of parodies, but it seems that only one, 'Request to Leda' (no. 136), was written by Thomas.

125. December 1938. In a letter to Vernon Watkins of this date (*Letters to Vernon Watkins*, p. 52). First published in *Wales*, vi–vii, p. 196, March 1939. (*Collected Poems* no. 52.)

126. January 1939. In a letter to Vernon Watkins of this date (*Letters to Vernon Watkins*, p. 56). First published in *Twentieth Century Verse*, XV–XVI, p. 149, February 1939. (*Collected Poems* no. 44.)

127. Early in March 1939. Enclosed in a letter to Vernon Watkins of this date (*Letters to Vernon Watkins*, p. 58) and first published in *Poetry, London*, II, p. 25, April 1939. (*Collected Poems* no. 58.) Llewelyn, Thomas's eldest son, was born on 30th January 1939. The poem is a dialogue between the child (stanzas I to III) and the mother (stanzas IV to VI).

128. May 1939. There is evidence for this date in a letter to Vernon Watkins (*Letters to Vernon Watkins*, p. 66). First published in *Seven*, VI, p. 5, Autumn 1939, as the first of 'Three Poems'. (*Collected Poems* no. 64.)

129. Autumn 1939. First published in *Life and Letters To-day*, XXIII, 26, pp. 60–8, October 1939, with the title 'Poem (to Caitlin)'. Revised for *Deaths and Entrances* (7th February 1946). (*Collected Poems* no. 66.) Vernon Watkins seems to have made a mistake in his note to a letter sent to him by Thomas on 5th June 1940 (*Letters to Vernon Watkins*, pp. 91ff). The poem referred to by Thomas in that letter and enclosed with it is not 'Unluckily for a death', but 'Into her lying down head' (see no. 135).

130. Autumn 1939. This is the date of first publication in *Seven*, VI, p. 6, as the second of 'Three Poems'. It is in *Deaths and Entrances* (p. 23), but not in *Collected Poems*.

131. Autumn 1939. This is the date of first publication in *Seven*, VI, p. 7, as the third of 'Three Poems'. (*Collected Poems* no. 78.)

132. January 1940. The poem was mentioned in a letter sent to Vernon Watkins at the end of January (*Letters to Vernon Watkins*, pp. 77–8). First publication was in *Life and Letters To-day*, XXIV, 31, pp. 274–5, March 1940. (*Collected Poems*, no. 77.)

133. February 1940. This poem was unfinished at the time when Thomas spoke of it in a letter to Vernon Watkins at the end of January (*Letters to Vernon Watkins*, p. 78), but was finished soon afterwards and sent to Watkins. First published in *Horizon*, I, 5, pp. 318–19, May 1940. (*Collected Poems* no. 73.)

134. March 1940. Thomas sent this satirical poem—this 'half comic attack upon myself', as he calls it—to Vernon Watkins on 19th March 1940 to be typed (*Letters to Vernon Watkins*, pp. 85–90). It was published, apparently for the first and only time, in *Cambridge Front*, I, pp. 8–9, Summer 1940. Thomas writes: 'The whole thing's bristling with intentional awkwardnesses, grotesque jokes, vulgarities of phrasing . . . it's not the sort of poem to try to polish; in fact, I've tried to avoid most slicknesses, which might have come so easily.'

135. May 1940. The poem was sent to Vernon Watkins for typing on 5th June 1940 (*Letters to Vernon Watkins*, pp. 93–5). First published in *Life and Letters To-day*, XXVII, 39, pp. 124–6, November 1940. (*Collected Poems* no. 68.)

136. August 1940. Thomas stayed with John Davenport at Marshfield during this month (FitzGibbon: *The Life of Dylan Thomas*, pp. 275ff.; *Letters to Vernon Watkins*, pp. 97ff.) and collaborated with him in writing *The Death of the King's Canary* (see note 124). In July 1942 a whole number of *Horizon* was devoted to William Empson (vol. VI, no. 31) and 'Request to Leda' appeared in it (p. 6), with the subtitle 'Homage to William Empson'.

137. August 1940. Mentioned in a letter to Vernon Watkins of this date (*Letters to Vernon Watkins*, p. 100), the poem was first published in *Horizon*, III, 13, pp. 12–13, January 1941. (*Collected Poems* no. 70).

138. 15th January 1941. This is the date of first publication in *Poetry, London*, IV, 91. Five years later, the poem underwent some revision for publication in *Deaths and Entrances* (p. 23). (*Collected Poems* no. 72.)

139. April 1941. A letter to John Davenport (*Selected Letters*, p. 249) suggests that the poem was finished by the end of April. First published in *Horison*, IV, 19, pp. 9–12, July 1941. (*Collected Poems* no. 82.)

140. May–June 1941. This is the date of first publication in *Poetry, London*, VI, pp. 186–7. (*Collected Poems* no. 65.)

141. July 1941. This poem has a long and complicated history, which begins with a version showing only remote resemblance, dated 22nd March 1933 in the *Buffalo Notebook*. Many revisions were made subsequently, but the text sent to Vernon Watkins in July 1941 (*Letters to Vernon Watkins*, pp. 107ff.) may be regarded as the final version. First published in *Life and Letters To-day*, XXXI, 50, pp. 42–3, October 1941. *Collected Poems* no. 74.)

142. 16th July 1941. An earlier poem, dated 9th May 1932 in the *Buffalo Notebook*, was transformed by extensive revision into a new composition; this final version, copied into the same Notebook, is dated 16th July 1941 by Thomas himself. First published in *Life and Letters To-day*, XXXI, 50, pp. 41–2, October 1941. (*Collected Poems* no. 67.) Though the details in this poem ('Sunday sombre bell', 'chained cup', 'fountain basin', 'rockery stones', 'nurses and swans') could apply to almost any park, this particular park is undoubtedly Cwmdonkin, not far from the Thomas house. There was, indeed, a hunchback who seemed to have nowhere else to go, who stayed from the moment the park opened until it closed. Cwmdonkin Park was a favourite haunt of truants from Swansea Grammar School, because it was bordered on one

side by a road that led directly to the school, but sometimes didn't. Thomas and I often met there to read poems to one another or write them, when, perhaps, we should have been learning Geography. But usually our amusements were more boisterous and less 'cultured'. (See 'Return Journey' in *Quite Early One Morning*, pp. 89–90.)

143. August 1941. This is the date of first publication in *Life and Letters To-day*, XXX, 48, p. 116. (*Collected Poems* no. 79.)

144. May 1944. First published on that date in *Our Time*, III, 10, p. 10. (*Collected Poems* no. 76.)

145. June 1944. First published in *Poetry, London*, IX, p. 34, undated but probably June 1944; this date can be conjectured from the dates of volumes VIII and X.

145. June 1944. The poem 'Thy breath was shed' which Thomas describes as 'very bad indeed' in a letter to Pamela Hansford Johnson (2nd May 1934, *Selected Letters*, p. 116) was considerably revised ten years later. In this new form it appears after 'Last night I dived my beggar arm' (see the previous note) on page 34 of *Poetry, London*, IX (undated, but probably June 1944).

147. August 1944. On 30th August Thomas sent the poem to Vernon Watkins (*Letters to Vernon Watkins*, pp. 115ff.); Watkins writes that the poem 'had been contemplated for three years'. First published in *Horizon*, XI, 62, pp. 82–3, February 1945. (*Collected Poems* no. 62.)

148. 21st September 1944. Thomas liked writing verse letters. This example, sent from New Quay, Cardiganshire, to T. W. Earp in Kingsley, Hampshire (*Selected Letters*, p. 267), is a parody of Earp's own verses. When Earp, art critic, French scholar, lovable eccentric and hypochondriac (sciatica), solemnly read aloud the verses of his anagrammed protégé, Pera, no one ventured to laugh. In crabbed style, twisted syntax, far-fetched rhymes and vertiginous *enjambement*, 'young' Pera out-Browninged, out-Cloughed them all. He was capable of writing, and indeed did write the line:

'Embrace, my Sheba she-bear, me', which fortunately is the only trace persisting in my memory from Pera's extensive œuvre. Here, with a foreshadowing of Llareggub, Thomas has out-Pera'd Earp.

149. November 1944. This poem was enclosed in a letter from New Quay, dated 15th November 1944, to Vernon Watkins (*Letters to Vernon Watkins*, p. 121). First published in *Horizon*, XI, 61, pp. 8–13, January 1945. (*Collected Poems* no. 81.) Many of the 'metaphysical' poets, as Dr Johnson called them (*Life of Cowley*), notably Quarles and Herbert, were fond of shaping their stanzas in fanciful geometric patterns, for example, in the shape of altars, wings and hour-glasses. George Puttenham, in *The Arte of English Poesie* (1589), devotes a long chapter to such figures as 'the fuzie or spindle, the pilaster, the piramis, the egge displayed, the tricquet reverst, the lozange rabbated' (Arber Reprint, pp. 104ff.). In this poem Thomas ingeniously contrives to create a mirror image of the first part (six 'lozanges') in the second (six 'tricquets displayed').

150. November 1944. Enclosed in a letter to Vernon Watkins, dated 28th November 1944 (*Letters to Vernon Watkins*, p. 123). First published in *Horizon*, XI, 61, p. 14, January 1945. (*Collected Poems* no. 83.)

151. March 1945. Sent with a letter to Vernon Watkins on 28th March 1945 (*Letters to Vernon Watkins*, p. 125). First published in *Poetry, Chicago*, LXVI, pp. 175–80. July 1945. (*Collected Poems* no. 71.)

152. March 1945. Enclosed in a letter to Vernon Watkins dated 28th March 1945 (*Letters to Vernon Watkins*, p. 128). First published in *New Republic*, CXII, 20, p. 675, 14th May 1945. (*Collected Poems* no. 61.)

153. March 1945. Sent with a letter to Vernon Watkins on 28th March 1945 (*Letters to Vernon Watkins*, p. 128). First published in *Life and Letters To-day*, XLVI, 95, pp. 28–9, July 1945. (*Collected Poems* no. 63.)

154. March 1945. Enclosed in a letter to Vernon Watkins dated

28th March 1945 (*Letters to Vernon Watkins*, p. 128). The original title was 'The Conversation of Prayers', as in the first publication (*Life and Letters To-day*, XLVI, 95, p. 29, July 1945). This was changed to 'The Conversation of Prayer' in *Deaths and Entrances* (p. 7). (*Collected Poems* no. 60.)

155. June 1945. This is the date of first publication, in *Life and Letters To-day*, XLV, 94, p. 155. (*Collected Poems* no. 80.)

156. October 1945. This is the date of first publication, in *Horizon*, XII, 70, pp. 221–2. (*Collected Poems* no. 84.) The phrase 'once below a time' (line 7) is used in an earlier poem (no. 132).

157. October 1945. This is the date of first publication, in *Life and Letters To-day*, XLVII, 98, p. 31. (*Collected Poems* no. 75.)

158. December 1947. This is the date of first publication, in *Horizon*, XVI, 96, pp. 302–5. (*Collected Poems* no. 85.) This is one of the 'In Country Heaven' poems; see note (*a*).

159. May 1949. This is the date of first publication, in *Botteghe Oscure*, IV, pp. 397–9. (*Collected Poems* no. 86.) One of the 'In Country Heaven' poems; see note (*a*). In Laugharne, Carmarthenshire, where Thomas lived, Sir John's Hill overlooks the estuary at a point to the east where the river Towy enters it. The whole area is a haunt of water-birds and birds of prey. It is hardly necessary to point out the importance of the influence of this environment upon Thomas in his later poems. An analysis of the structure of 'Over Sir John's Hill' will be found at the end of the Note on Verse-Patterns (p. 247).

160. September 1950. At the time of the broadcast on 25th September 1950 (*Quite Early One Morning*, p. 155) this poem had not been printed; it was still 'waiting for someone who prints strikingly few copies, at impossible prices, on fine soft Cashmere goat's hair'. It was 'In the White Giant's Thigh' and not 'Over Sir John's Hill' (as stated in *Quite Early One Morning*, p. 181) that first appeared in *Botteghe Oscure* in November 1950 (no. VI, pp. 335–7). 'Over Sir John's Hill' had been printed a year before in *Botteghe Oscure* (see note

159). This is one of the 'In Country Heaven' poems; see note (*a*). (*Collected Poems* no. 89.) There are fifteen regular quatrains in this poem; their division by irregular spacing is clearly intentional. In a similar way, Thomas divided the quatrains of his unfinished 'Elegy' (note '*b*') into groups of three lines each, making the fragment look—at a quick glance and quite wrongly—like *terza rima*. In both poems, the intention is evidently to 'overlay' contradictory patterns.

161. March 1951. In a letter to Princess Caetani, dated 20th March 1951, Thomas says that this poem is 'nearly finished' (*Selected Letters*, p. 353). It was first published in Marguerite Caetani's *Botteghe Oscure* in November 1951 (VIII, pp. 209–210). (*Collected Poems* no. 88.)

162. May 1951. The poem was enclosed in a letter to Princess Caetani on 28th May 1951 (*Selected Letters*, p. 359); the letter has a postscript: 'The only person I can't show the little enclosed poem to is, of course, my father, who doesn't know he's dying.' D. J. Thomas lingered for more than a year after this, and died on 15th December 1952. The poem was first published in *Botteghe Oscure*, VIII, p. 208, November 1951. (*Collected Poems* no. 69.) It is significant that for this subject and for this occasion, Thomas deliberately chose to discipline himself by the use of a strict form, the villanelle.

163. Summer 1951. The date of first publication is October 1951, in *World Review* (New Series), XXXII, pp. 66–7 (*Collected Poems* no. 87). The eighth line ('His driftwood thirty-fifth wind turned age'), which suggests the date 27th October 1949, is misleading. The poem was written after Thomas's return from Persia, when he spent the summer in Laugharne (FitzGibbon: *The Life of Dylan Thomas*, p. 366).

(*a*) In his broadcast of 25th September 1950 (*Quite Early One Morning*, pp. 155ff.), Thomas spoke of a long 'poem in preparation'. Three sections of this had been completed with the titles: 'In Country Sleep', 'Over Sir John's Hill' and 'In the White Giant's Thigh'. The first two, dating from 1947 and 1949, had already been printed, while the last was still in manuscript (see notes 158, 159, 160). He disclosed the 'grand and simple' plan of the long poem: 'The poem is to be called "In Country Heaven". The godhead, the author, the milky-way farmer, the first cause, architect, lamp-lighter, quintessence, the beginning Word, the anthropomorphic bowler-out and blackballer, the stuff of all men, scapegoat, martyr, maker, woe-bearer—He, on top of a hill in heaven, weeps whenever, outside that state of being called his country, one of his worlds drops dead, vanishes screaming, shrivels, explodes, murders itself. And, when he weeps, Light and his tears glide down together, hand in hand. So, at the beginning of the projected poem, he weeps, and Country Heaven is suddenly dark. Bushes and owls blow out like candles. And the countrymen of heaven crouch all together under the hedges and, among themselves in the tear-salt darkness, surmise which world, which star, which of their late, turning homes in the skies has gone for ever. And this time, spreads the heavenly hedgerow rumour, it is the Earth. The Earth has killed itself. It is black, petrified, wizened, poisoned, burst; insanity has blown it rotten; and no creatures at all, joyful, despairing, cruel, kind, dumb, afire, loving, dull, shortly and brutishly hunt their days down like enemies on that corrupted face. And, one by one, those heavenly hedgerow-men who once were of the Earth call to one another, through the long night, Light and His tears falling, what they remember, what they sense in the submerged wilderness and on the exposed hair's breadth of the mind, what they feel trembling on the nerves of a nerve, what they know in their Edenie hearts, of that self-called place. They remember places, fears, loves, exaltation, misery, animal joy, ignorance, and mysteries, all *we* know and do not know. The poem is made of these tellings. And the poem becomes, at last, an affirmation of the beautiful and terrible worth of the Earth. It grows into a praise of what is and what could be on this lump in the skies. It is a poem about happiness.' (*Quite Early One Morning*, p. 156.)

Thomas continued to work on the long poem, but did not live to finish it. The fragments of 'In Country Heaven' clearly form a part of the opening section; this is the title-poem, and, according to the design of the whole work, the beginning of it. Some lines had already been composed at the time of the broadcast: 'Light and his tears glide down together . . . Bushes and owls blow out like candles.' But the assured tone of Thomas's statements in his broadcast may be misleading. The idea of writing a long work of this kind did not begin with 'In Country Sleep' (1947); it suggested itself gradually and was often abandoned. Thomas wished to share, with radio listeners or with friends, his enthusiasm for the planning of a long poem. No one now can tell how firmly he would have held to this purpose; no one can tell whether he privately believed his abilities to be of the kind to fulfil it successfully (see FitzGibbon: *The Life of Dylan Thomas*, pp. 326ff.). The fact that the four poems differ in verse structure is unimportant. What is more important and striking is Thomas's apparent indifference about the order in which the poems should be read. The order of composition of the completed poems is: 158 (1947), 159 (1949), 160 (1950). In the broadcast of 1950, they are read by the poet himself in this order: 159, 158, 160. The order chosen by Thomas in his collected poems two years later is: 158 (*Collected Poems* no. 85), 159 (no. 86), and then, after two poems of totally different character, 160 (no. 89). In a letter to Oscar Williams on 28th May 1951 (*Selected Letters*, p. 360), Thomas implies that 'In the White Giant's Thigh' is the opening section; in reply to a question of Bill McAlpine about the position of the same poem, Thomas said that he had not made up his mind: 'but it'll fit in somewhere' (FitzGibbon: *The Life of Dylan Thomas*, p. 328).

The version of 'In Country Heaven' printed here is based on manuscripts in the Library of the University of Texas. Many other versions, of course, could be put together from the same material, and would be equally 'authentic'. The greatest number of variants occur in the five lines beginning 'Light and his tears glide down together', where there are so many divergences that it is impossible to combine them in a readable text. Apart from this, the version printed here is solidly based down to the line 'Pity for death'. Tentative or conjectural continuations of the poem after this line have been omitted.

(b) The poet's father, D. J. Thomas, died on 15th December 1952. Dylan Thomas left this Elegy unfinished at the time of his own death, on 9th November 1953. The version printed here was made by Vernon Watkins and first published in *Encounter*, XXIX, pp. 30–1, February 1956. The first seventeen lines, arranged in threes and ending '. . . to the roots of the sea', are as Thomas left them. 'Of the added lines,' Watkins writes, 'sixteen are exactly as Dylan Thomas wrote them, and the remainder are only altered to the extent of an inversion or one or two words. Their order might well have been different. The poem might also have been made much longer.' (Note in *Encounter*.) The grouping into stanzas of three lines cuts across the basic quatrain pattern (cf. no. 160).

(i) December 1925, when the poem was printed in the *Swansea Grammar School Magazine*, p. 74. Thomas, born on 27th October 1914, wrote this poem when he was eleven years of age.

(ii) 1928. Printed in the *Swansea Grammar School Magazine*, March 1928, p. 19.

(iii) Summer 1928. Printed in the *Swansea Grammar School Magazine*, July 1928, p. 43.

(iv) Autumn 1928. Printed in the *Swansea Grammar School Magazine*, December 1928, p. 77.

(v) February 1929. Musical setting for soloists, chorus and orchestra; the musical manuscript in my possession. First printed in the *Swansea Grammar School Magazine*, March 1929, pp. 15–16.

(vi) 20th April 1929. Musical setting; music manuscript in my possession.

(vii) 28th April 1929. Musical setting; music manuscript in my possession.

(viii) 28th April 1929. Musical setting; music manuscript in my possession.

(ix) April–May 1929. Musical setting; music manuscript in my possession.

(x) 5th May 1929. Musical setting; music manuscript in my possession.

(xi) 7th May 1929. Musical setting; music manuscript in my possession.

(xii) 2nd November 1929, with the title 'Little Idyll'. Musical setting; music manuscript in my possession. First printed, unsigned, with the title 'To the Spring-Spirit', in the *Swansea Grammar School Magazine*, December 1929, p. 77.

(xiii) November 1929. Musical setting; music manuscript in my possession. First printed, unsigned, in the *Swansea Grammar School Magazine*, December 1929, p. 88.

(xiv) Dated 6th May 1930 in the *Buffalo Notebook*. The Notebook is headed 'Mainly Free Verse Poems'. Text in British Museum Add. MSS. 48217.

(xv) May–June 1930. The date may be conjectured from the position of the poem in British Museum Add. MSS. 48217.

(xvi) Dated June 6th (1930) in the *Buffalo Notebook*. As in some other poems written at about the same time, there is no punctuation at the end. This was very 'modern' and Cummings-like.

(xvii) Dated June 19th (1930) in the *Buffalo Notebook*.

(xviii) Dated 1st July 1930 in the *Buffalo Notebook*. Text in British Museum Add. MSS. 48217.

(xix) Dated July 17th (1930) in the *Buffalo Notebook*.

(xx) Dated 8th August 1930 in the *Buffalo Notebook*. Text in British Museum Add. MSS. 48217.

(xxi) Part of this poem, written in the previous year (April 1929), was copied out for purposes of revision into the 1930 *Buffalo Notebook* shortly after the composition of no. (xx), and two more sections were added. For this reason, 'Woman on Tapestry' can be tentatively dated August 1930.

There are many indications that Thomas intended to write a much longer poem, and to revise still further what he had already written. But during this fertile period, the patience necessary for revision, which later on characterized him, was lacking; he preferred to pass on quickly to the next poem.

The text of 'Woman on Tapestry' is obviously imperfect. The use of the personal pronouns, for example, seems inconsistent. In stanza VII, the second person intrudes without warning, and a case could be made out for changing this to the third person, as in the rest of the poem. In spite of the rather garbled text, 'Woman on Tapestry' is included because it is so representative of the poet's style of writing at this time.

Thomas had ample opportunity of seeing tapestry, because whenever he called at my home—that is, nearly every day—he found himself surrounded by it. My mother was a very skilled 'worker in wools' (see 'The Fight' in *Portrait of the Artist as a Young Dog*). One series of eight Jacobean panels, each six by four feet, she called 'The Garden of Eden'. The strange conventions of a landscape that never was, with speckled hills and slim, twining stems covered with fantastic fruit and birds, are suggested by several passages in the poem; for example:

'And the roots of the trees climbed through the air
Touching the silver clouds . . . the hills
Coiled into their bodies like snakes.'

(xxii) August 1930. The date may be conjectured from the position of the poem in British Museum Add. MSS. 48217.

(xxiii) Though without date in the *Buffalo Notebook*, it can be conjectured that this poem was written in the late summer of 1930. I have changed the original 'who' in line 4 to 'that', as in the first line, and have deleted a full stop in line 13.

(xxiv) September 1930. The date may be conjectured from the position of the poem in British Museum Add. MSS. 48217.

(xxv) No date is given in the *Buffalo Notebook*, but it can be conjectured that the poem was written in the early autumn of 1930.

(xxvi) Autumn 1930. The date may be conjectured from the position of the poem in British Museum Add. MSS. 48217.

A PUB POEM

September 1943. Thomas often amused himself by writing doggerel in pubs. In this book examples have been given of his serious poetry, immature and mature, his occasional verse, parody, unfinished sketches and juvenilia. For the sake of completeness, this amusing specimen of doggerel is included to represent the 'pub poetry'. 'Sooner than you can water milk' was written in a pub where Thomas had arranged to meet his friend Wynford Vaughan Thomas. The beer flowed freely during its composition and the handwriting in the manuscript deteriorates badly. The last couplet, in fact, is almost entirely illegible. Vaughan Thomas writes: 'The last two lines only come back to me through Dylan's remembered voice.' It was Vaughan Thomas who discovered the poem only recently, quite by accident, and it now appears here in publication for the first time. 'Cards', by the way, is short for Cardiganshire.

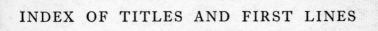

INDEX OF TITLES AND FIRST LINES

INDEX OF TITLES AND FIRST LINES

The figures are poem numbers, not page numbers

Everyman
A selection of titles

*indicates volumes available in paperback

Complete lists of Everyman's Library and Everyman Paperbacks
are available from the Sales Department, J.M. Dent and Sons Ltd,
Aldine House,33 Welbeck Street, London WIM 8LX.

BIOGRAPHY

Bligh, William. *A Book of the 'Bounty'*
Boswell, James. *The Life of Samuel Johnson*
Byron, Lord. *Letters*
Cibber, Colley. *An Apology for the Life of Colley Cibber*
*De Quincey, Thomas. *Confessions of an English Opium-Eater*
Forster, John. *Life of Charles Dickens* (2 vols)
*Gaskell, Elizabeth. *The Life of Charlotte Brontë*
*Gilchrist, Alexander. *The Life of William Blake*
Houghton, Lord. *The Life and Letters of John Keats*
*Johnson, Samuel. *Lives of the English Poets: a selection*
Pepys, Samuel. *Diary* (3 vols)
Thomas, Dylan
    **Adventures in the Skin Trade*
    **Portrait of the Artist as a Young Dog*
Tolstoy. *Childhood, Boyhood and Youth*
*Vasari, Giorgio. *Lives of the Painters, Sculptors, and Architects*
    (4 vols)

ESSAYS AND CRITICISM

Arnold, Matthew. *On the Study of Celtic Literature*
*Bacon, Francis. *Essays*
Coleridge, Samuel Taylor
    **Biographia Literaria*
    Shakespearean Criticism (2 vols)
Dryden, John. *Of Dramatic Poesy and other critical essays*
    (2 vols)

*Lawrence, D.H. *Stories, Essays and Poems*
*Milton, John. *Prose Writings*
Montaigne, Michel Eyquem de. *Essays* (3 vols)
Paine, Thomas. *The Rights of Man*
Pater, Walter. *Essays on Literature and Art*
Spencer, Herbert. *Essays on Education and Kindred Subjects*

FICTION

*American Short Stories of the Nineteenth Century
Austen, Jane
  Emma
  Mansfield Park
  Northanger Abbey
  Persuasion
  Pride and Prejudice
  Sense and Sensibility
*Bennett, Arnold. *The Old Wives' Tale*
Boccaccio, Giovanni. *The Decameron*
Brontë, Anne
  Agnes Grey
  The Tenant of Wildfell Hall
Brontë, Charlotte
  Jane Eyre
  The Professor and *Emma* (a fragment)
  Shirley
  Villette
Brontë, Emily. *Wuthering Heights* and *Poems*
*Bunyan, John. *Pilgrim's Progress*
Butler, Samuel.
  Erewhon and *Erewhon Revisited*
  The Way of All Flesh
Collins, Wilkie
  The Moonstone
  The Woman in White
Conrad, Joseph
  The Nigger of the 'Narcissus', Typhoon, Falk and other stories
  Nostromo

*Stowe, Harriet Beecher. *Uncle Tom's Cabin*
Stevenson, R.L.
  *Dr Jekyll and Mr Hyde, The Merry Men and other tales
  *Kidnapped
  *The Master of Ballantrae and *Weir of Hermiston*
  *Treasure Island
Swift, Jonathan
  *Gulliver's Travels
  *A Tale of a Tub and other satires
Thackeray, W.M.
  Henry Esmond
  *Vanity Fair
Thomas, Dylan
  *Miscellany 1
  *Miscellany 2
  *Miscellany 3
*Tolstoy, Leo. *Master and Man and other parables and tales*
Trollope, Anthony
  *The Warden
  *Barchester Towers
  Dr Thorne
  *Framley Parsonage
  Small House at Allington
  Last Chronicle of Barset
*Voltaire, *Candide and other tales*
*Wilde, Oscar. *The Picture of Dorian Gray*
Woolf, Virginia. *To the Lighthouse*

HISTORY

*The Anglo-Saxon Chronicle
Burnet, Gilbert. *History of His Own Time*
*Crèvecoeur. *Letters from an American Farmer*
Gibbon, Edward. *The Decline and Fall of the Roman Empire*
    (6 vols)
Macaulay, T.B. *The History of England* (4 vols)
Machiavelli, Niccolò. *Florentine History*
Prescott, W.H. *History of the Conquest of Mexico*